# ONE FOOT IN THE GRAVE

## MY LIFE ON AN ARTIFICIAL LEG

**Don Addor**

Front Cover: My girlfriend Joan McDonald and I shortly after my return to the States in the late Spring of 1945. I was a patient at Walter Reed Army Hospital waiting for a "clean-up" operation on my stump and the long awaited issue of the prosthesis. I think the photo was taken during a picnic at Rock Creek Park, Wash., D.C.

Order this book online at www.trafford.com
or email orders@trafford.com

Most Trafford titles are also available at major online book retailers.

Printed in the United States of America.

ISBN: 978-1-4269-6815-0 (sc)
ISBN: 978-1-4269-6816-7 (hc)
ISBN: 978-1-4269-6817-4 (e)

Library of Congress Control Number: 2011907049

*Trafford rev. 06/03/2011*

 www.trafford.com

North America & international
toll-free: 1 888 232 4444 (USA & Canada)
phone: 250 383 6864 ♦ fax: 812 355 4082

# Contents

from the beginning until the present that I have had or done as an amputee who has done pretty well on his prosthesis.

I would like to point out that I did not set out to do any great things on my new leg. I just did the best I could with what came in front of me along my path of life. I was often surprised to find myself doing what I was doing.

# Chapter One

# How I Lost My Leg

I lost my right leg above the knee early Christmas morning in the year 1944. I was in an Army hospital in Paris after having been wounded in the defense of Bastogne, Belgium during the "Battle of the Bulge".

As a member of the 20th Armored Infantry Battalion of the 10th Armored Division we had been among the first to arrive at Bastogne following the German attack in the Ardenes. We arrived in Bastogne late at night after a two-day road trip from down in Metz, France. We were directed to a long warehouse type building and told to get some sleep. I had just unrolled my homemade sleeping bag when orders came from a first lieutenant to mount up again.

It was back to the Major's half-track and off into the foggy wet night. The fog was so thick that we could only make about three miles per hour. I was standing up through the half-track's fifty caliber machine gun ring mount leaning forward as far as I could trying to figure out which way the big truck just ahead of us in see what would happen as the tank was not on fire. However another volley of artillery came screaming in and exploding among the tree branches and I headed back toward the end of the column as fast as I could go.

This wasn't very fast for when I tried to run with a low profile to get under the machine gun fire that was coming out of the fog on my right flank, I would step on the tail of my overcoat and fall flat on my face. I finally had to stop and wiggle out of it. Once shed of that long coat I crawled over to the shallow ditch that ran along the edge of the road. It wasn't much of a ditch, but it did give a little cover. The other side of the road where the enemy fire was coming from was much better. It had a bank of dirt about four feet high running along the edge of the road.

We were now under heavy small arms rifle and machine gun fire. The chances of getting across the road were slim. The bodies of about ten fellow GI's laying scattered out there told me not here and not now. Sections of the road were red with their blood. I slithered on my belly into that shallow "grove" and joined a long line of others who were inching their way back to the end of our column to regroup. I was one of the last in this line as I had been very close to the head of our column when we were ambushed.

It wasn't great protection, but if you kept your self real flat and inched back the bullets cleared your back by three or four inches. You could feel the heat from the tracers. I was moving back slowly when they sent mortar and artillery fire. Both sides of the street were lined with large trees. The shells exploded over us in the tree limbs showering the area with shrapnel. Hot jagged pieces of iron hit all around me, but none hit me. There was a medic under the big tree about fifteen feet in front of me. He had been putting a dressing on a leg wound when the shells burst over us.

He was not lucky. I saw him jump up and he called to his fellow medic across the road. "Charley! I've been hit." He started to run across the road, but only got half way. There he fell on his face dead, blood still spurting out of a great hole that went clean through his chest. I knew I had just seen a dead man running. The soldier he had been working on was also dead. I started to move again back down the ditch. My feet hit the head of the man behind me. I tapped his helmet with my foot and hollered, "Let's move it!"

He didn't move. I kicked his helmet harder and he still didn't move. As I crawled over him I realized that that tree burst had also killed him. I looked at him closer and saw that he was the officer that had written me up for a Silver Star yesterday after I had stopped a Tiger tank from entering Noville. There was another burst of small arms fire and I started making my way down the ditch again. There was no one behind me now so I could crawl faster.

I looked at the other side of the road. That bank sure looked like good protection. I noticed that I was almost to a destroyed army truck in the center of the road. There was a place where I could cross over. I ran to the other side stepping over a couple of dead bodies of men who had not made it. I slide in to the ditch and stretched my arms and legs. I sat with my back to the edge of the ditch with a mound of half melted snow as a pillow. I looked up the road towards Foy, but could only see a little past that knocked out truck. It was the same in all directions. Fog, like trying to see through a white blanket. I looked to my right and saw Captain Geiger sitting there talking to another officer.

I heard a shell explode in the other direction. I looked to see where it hit and when I looked back Captain Geiger and the other officer had disappeared. I looked all around me and found that except for the dead I was all alone. Well, not quite. There was still a hell of a lot of Germans out there in the fog. The firing had slowed down to almost nothing, but I knew that they would soon be coming out of the fog right at me, or where I was. It was time to get out of here, and fast.

The plan of retreat was to pull back and move over land from our right flank and into Bastogne. I ran back to the other side of the street trotting along the edge of the road looking for footprints and vehicle tracks in the snow and mud. I was careful to keep the line of disabled vehicles between the enemy and me. They both made good concealment and cover. Not far down the road I saw a place where there was a considerable amount of disturbance in the ground.

I thought, "This must be the place!"

I was wrong. I had only gone a few yards out into the fog when there was a blast near by. I was blown into the air and landed face down in the mud. My helmet went in one direction and my rifle in another. I was conscious, but numb all over. I couldn't move any part of my body. There was also a great ringing in my ears. I looked out across the muddy grass and saw the cause of my discomfort. Just a couple of feet to my left was a big hole and in the center of it the tail of a mortar shell stuck out of the mud. It was still smoking. It was so close that I could almost reach out and grab it. If I could move and wanted the damn thing.

Slowly the feeling began to return to my body. First I could move my legs and then my arms and the rest of my body regained its feeling. Not all of it, but I could move. I checked myself out and the only wound I found was a piece of shrapnel in my back. When I ran my hand down my back I could feel it sticking through my field jacket in the small of my back about an inch from my backbone. It wasn't bleeding and it didn't hurt. I could just feel it sticking in me. I was lucky the soft earth of this cow pasture had buried most of the shrapnel.

I looked ahead of me and saw my M-1. I got up half way and heading for it. However, I had only taken three steps when I heard the chatter of a burp gun and a mess of bullets flew by.

I felt them tear through the back of my field jacket. One singed the end of my nose, but the ones that did the damage were the three that went through my right leg at the calf. I was running bent as low as I could. My right leg was out in front when they hit and went through. I saw them come out the other side or rather the stream of blood that followed their path.

Two went right through the bone, but didn't shatter it. They must have been armor piercing. The other one went right through the artery. I could tell by the way my blood spurted out on the green grass. I went down hitting the ground hard. I said to myself, "This is it. You've had it." Being hit twice in a couple of minutes kind of wipes one out. I lay there and said goodbye to Mom and Dad and my girlfriend, Joan. I waited but no trumpets or bright lights. Instead I heard a voice say, "you're not dead yet." I don't know where the voice came from, but I heard it.

I pulled off my belt and put it around my leg at the knee and pulled it as tight as I could. It slowed the bleeding a little. I cut the straps off the bandoleer of ammo that had been around my shoulder. I stuck my combat knife back under the belt and twisted. The blood stopped. This was good. I tried to tie it in place with the straps from the bandoleer, but laying flat on my side I couldn't make it stay. This was bad. Back in the States during self-aid class it had worked fine, but I had been sitting up during those dry runs. Here, if I tried to sit up someone would shoot at me, or something like the mine rack on a burning vehicle near by would explode with a hot piece of iron passing close over head. I had been singed twice by such explosions.

I lay there holding that knife in a tight position. I was getting weaker and my hand would slip off and the blood would fly again. My whole pant leg and shoe was full of it. The sight of the spurting would revive me and my hold, but I knew if I didn't do something soon, I was doomed.

I picked up the clip with my free hand and pulled the bullets out of it with my teeth. I then inserted them under the belt around my leg. As each bullet was slipped into place the bleeding lessened until it stopped.

I pulled the knife out from under the belt and my "bullet" tourniquet still worked. Now I looked around and there I was in this Belgium cow pasture surrounded by fog and all alone. I crawled over to where my rifle was and picked it up. It was a bit muddy so I cleaned the mud off the vital places and checked that it was in working order.

We knew the Germans were not taking prisoners, even if they could walk, and I sure was a litter case. So I figured if they came I would go out shooting and maybe I could kill a couple before they finished me off. No big hero stuff. I was just not one to lie still and wait to be killed.

I lay there in the fog waiting for whatever might happen. Once a German patrol was almost upon me, but turned and ran back into the fog yelling something in German. I had the point man in my sights when they turned back. Time really drags in such a situation. It seemed like hours had gone by when I heard a vehicle coming up the road. I turned and watched it. It was one of our jeeps with two guys in our uniforms in it, but during this battle one could not be sure as the enemy was using our stuff too. They stopped and looked at one of the dead guys in the road and took his dog tags. Their manner was not that of the enemy, so I gave holler for help.

I felt weak and didn't know if I could make enough noise to get their attention. My cry for help came out loud and clear through the damp air. They almost jumped out of their socks. They came running over to me. I knew one. He was Corporal Still, the Major's jeep driver. The other was a medic from the 101st Paratroopers. The medic checked my leg and I asked him for a shot of morphine. Nothing had hurt yet, but I was afraid it would start at any time and I still needed a clear head to get us out of this mess.

Corporal Still said they had gotten lost in the fog and had been dodging Germans for a day or more. When they finally found their way back to Noville no one was there. I told them what had happened and how the withdraw plan was supposed to work. They helped me to the jeep and Still turned it around.

We passed a tank and heard a moaning. Still and the medic pulled one of our guys out of the tank and laid him out on the hood as best they could. He recognized me and said "Hello." There was a small bit of bone missing from the middle of his forehead. It was not bleeding. In fact there was no other sign of injury showing on his body. This does not mean that there were no other wounds, just none we could see. When a tank gets hit, a mess of nuts, bolts and small pieces of steel go flying around the inside of the tank, often causing many small wounds…often fatal ones.

Not far down the road I saw the place where our Task Force had pulled off of the road to head for Bastogne. Corporal Still did the best he could to give us a smooth ride, but it was still pretty rough. However, we did not see any of the enemy. Apparently our troops in Bastogne were keeping them busy.

Finally through the thick fog we spotted a jeep parked under a big fir tree. The big Red Cross in its white field told us that it was a medic's vehicle. We pulled over to it and Doc Nefland greeted us. Doc was our battalion dentist, but spent most of his time in the middle of the fighting as sort of a super medic.

There were two corpsmen with him. While the "Doc" was putting a certified G.I. tourniquet on me I told him there were no more coming back. Only the dead remained out there blanketed by the fog. We followed the medics back into Bastogne. My friend on the hood had died so was dropped off at the quartermasters and I went on to our Battalion Aid Station.

It was in the basement of a large building that looked like it could have been some kind of dry goods store. They greeted me with a stretcher and down the stairs I went into a basement crowded with wounded. Our battalion surgeon came over to see what attention I needed. I said, "Hello Doc! It's my right leg again. I think I messed it up pretty good this time."

I had been having trouble with my right knee and had to wear an "ace" bandage on it most of the time. I passed out before I learned that this was a new Battalion surgeon. The one I had known became sick just before we went into battalion reserve. He was now recovering in a hospital in Paris.

I did not come to again until I woke up on a hospital train heading for Paris. I could not figure out where I was. It seemed to me like I was in some kind of a tunnel and there was a lot of rocking and roaring going on. I started to get up, but a medic put his hand on my shoulder and said, "Hey, soldier where do you think you're going?"

I responded, "Back to my outfit!"

He said, "Wrong! You're on a hospital train heading for Paris."

It was then that I saw the two bottles hanging above my head and the plastic tubes feeding me their "juice." I looked around again and saw that I was indeed on a train with stretchers in two or three tiers on each side. I did not pass out again. That stuff in those bottles did their job.

I did come to for a short time some where along my line of travel. I woke up in a large room in a big building. It had tile walls and hard floors. I looked to my left and saw that the person there had the blanket pulled over his head and a large yellow quartermaster tag on his big toe sticking out of the bottom of the blanket. He was dead.

I looked to my right and here too was a soldier with a blanket over his head and that yellow tag on his big toe. I eased up a bit to look around. Everyone in the room was dressed the same way. I looked down towards the end of my stretcher and there it was, a big yellow quartermaster tag tied snugly around the big toe of my right leg. I was in a temporary morgue!

I heard footsteps coming down the hall outside of the room. Once more I dug down deep for the strength to yell. Once again it came out like "Gangbusters!" An army nurse poked her head through the doorway. Her face was as white as her uniform. She saw me and said, "Don't move. I'll be right back!"

I thought that that was a stupid thing to say. If I could have moved I would have been long gone out of that door. I realized that she was under shock. It's not every day that some "body" in the morgue calls out to you.

She returned with two corpsmen who carried me out of that room and down the hall. There they set me down at the end of a long line of men on stretchers waiting for medical attention. The causalities from the Battle of the bulge were numerous to say the least.

My hospital train pulled into the station at Paris and I was off loaded onto a platform to wait my turn for an ambulance ride to the hospital. There was a top, but no sides to the loading dock. It was snowing and I watched the flakes of snow drift in under the roof and swirl down onto the blankets that covered me. There they would slowly melt away. I could hear traffic somewhere out there slushing through the snow.

My ambulance backed up to the platform and I was carried to it. A little old Frenchman and a matching lady opened the back doors and as they slid me in to the vehicle I realized that he and she were the drivers. That did not make me feel very secure. They both must have been in the Book of Records as the oldest couple alive on our planet.

However, he and his wife did an excellent job delivering us to the hospital through the thick icy slush and heavy snow. One of the ambulances did not make it, but slid into another vehicle and turned over. When we were unloaded I gave the little man a big "Merci Beaucoup!" I meant every word of it.

A ward man pushed my gurney down a long hall. I looked up and above me hanging from the ceiling were Christmas tree balls and tinsel. At a corner a life size cardboard Santa Clause was greeting me. I started to ask my pusher what day it was, but we pulled up next to an empty bed.

What a beautiful sight. A real bed with white sheets. It had been almost a year since I had seen one. They lifted me from the gurney and set me down on it. While one of them tucked me in a nurse stuck a thermometer in my mouth and told me not to talk. A doctor came and greeted me and asked me how I was. He went to the foot of my bed took a look at my chart and then gently lifted my leg up. At some time and place a cast had been put on it.

As he lifted my leg the plaster of the cast, now a gooey mess, sloshed on to my nice clean sheets. Along with this came a terrible smell. A smell like a thousand dead rats lying in the blazing sun. I looked at my toes sticking out from the cast. They were a bluish black. I knew that smell! It was the smell of dead rotting flesh.

I had gangrene! My leg was dead. I also knew that it meant that my leg would have to go. The doctor lowered my leg and came to see me. He stood there for a moment looking down at me with a grim expression on his face. I could see that he was struggling trying to tell me that he would have to amputate my leg.

I looked at him and sort of smiled. I said, "Gangrene? I guess it will have to go!"

He let out a sign of relief and answered, "Yes it will. I hate to remove it on Christmas morning."

I told him that if he had been where I had been, he would know that I was lucky to be alive and here in the hospital. I did not look at it as the loss of a leg, but as a gift of life. What better Christmas gift could I receive than life!

He looked a bit amazed and said he would send the Chaplain to see me. The Chaplain came and we had a nice talk. He too agreed with me that I was very lucky to be here. He led me in a prayer of thanks and then joined me in a prayer for my Mom and Dad and girlfriend Joan. Then I lay back in my beautiful bed and had the best night's sleep ever, or at least since a long time.

The next morning, very early, the gurney arrived at the side of my bed and I was off to the operating room. A medic began to cut the cast off of my leg and I asked him if I could watch. He said, "Sure if you really want to!"

I said, "I do" and he moved to give me a better view as he cut away at the plaster. I knew it would not be a pleasant sight, but it was my leg and I wanted to kind of wish it goodbye.

A nurse came to me and stuck a needle in my arm. She said, "count from ten backwards." I reached eight I think and never saw my messy leg. I was out like a light. The next thing I remembered was that I was back in my bed again and the nurse had just removed a thermometer from my mouth.

She held it up to the light so she could better read it. I said, "I bet it's high!"

She responded, "Why, no. It is almost normal."

I asked her why I felt so hot. She took a closer look at my bed and started to laugh. I wondered what was so funny about me lying in bed so hot and sweaty. She started to remove blankets. Heavy wool army blankets. There were seven of them that came off of my bed before my regular bedding was reached. I laughed too!

She explained that Paris was having a very white and cold Christmas. There was an open court in the center of the hospital that had to be crossed. Some one had been very careful in covering me so I wouldn't feel or get cold. I could not feel the weight of the blankets, as there was a wire cage over the lower portion of my body to keep them off of my operation.

She then asked me if I wanted a drink. I thought she meant water so I told her that I was not thirsty, but just hot! The nurse informed me that she did not mean that kind of drink and winked at me.

I said, "Oh, scotch and water would be nice."

She poured me one and then we toasted Christmas 1944! Actually I toasted the yuletide. She was on duty and could not join me, She said that the hospitals officers had saved their liquor ration so the patients could have this Christmas treat.

I did not stay at that hospital in Paris very long. The causalities from the Battle of the Bulge kept coming in and space was needed. I was put on another hospital train this time headed for Cherbourg. The same port that my outfit and I had entered France. I went across the English Channel in a small local fishing boat that had been converted to transport wounded in England.

The hold that once held the fish was now full of hospital beds. However, the smell of its former occupants lingered on. I'm glad that it was nice weather and the Channel waters were calm. It would have been a jarring experience otherwise. While we crossed over English attendants served us with a breakfast of bacon and fried eggs.

Boy! Did they look good. I had not seen any kind of eggs since we had left Camp Gordon, not even powdered. However, they looked better than they tasted. The British never did go in for much seasoning and these beautiful Sunnyside-up eggs had none at all. They were still greatly appreciated and were a sign that I had returned to civilization!

It was night when we made port at Southampton and were loaded on to a British hospital train. A conductor told us that we were headed for a hospital near Oxford. Shortly after the train started its journey to that well-known college town, our attendants came down the aisle handing out noisemakers and confetti. It was then that I realized that it was New Year's Eve. There was a large clock at one end of the railway car. As the last hour of 1944 faded away, the conductor led us in a countdown. When 1945 came aboard we all hollered and cheered and blew our horns. Confetti sailed through the air and the New Year was welcomed in as we sang the old one out with a few choruses of Auld Lang Syne.

My new home was a large Quonset hut with an old fashioned wood burning stove at each end. There were about 40 patients to each hut and one nurse to two huts and most were bed patients. I was told again that I would soon be heading home by air, but this never happened as the influx of wounded never slowed down and those with more serious wounds than I got those flights back to the good ole U.S.A.

At first I was a bit discouraged and mad at having to wait, as I was eager to get home and to see my family. I also wanted to show Mom that I was all right and would do ok with only one leg. I had written Mom and Dad while in Paris, but did not tell them that their son had lost his right leg. They got my letter before the army telegram that only said that I had shell wounds of the right leg. At least they got the leg correct.

I knew that my loss would upset Mom and Dad, but I also knew that when they heard my voice and I told them my story they would, like me, know that they were lucky that I had survived. The loss of only one leg and not my head would turn a bad situation into one of happiness and thanks. I knew that they would feel as I did, that my return was truly a miracle.

The next morning when the doctor made his rounds, they put my stump in skin traction. This pulled my skin down over the end of my stump. They glued a slip sock, an open tube of cloth, over my stump and dressing. Next a rope was tied to its end and at the end of the rope was a cloth bag that held weights. The bag of weights was dropped off of the end of the bed a bit above the floor and gravity did the rest.

This presented a problem as the weight not only pulled the skin down, but also pulled my body towards the end of my bed. It was particularly bad at nighttime. I was always waking up at night to fight my way back up to my pillow. I consoled myself by remembering that I healed fast so this ordeal would not last long.

During those first days in bed in England, I often wondered what it would be like and what I would be able to do with an artificial leg. I knew I would get around on it somehow, but to what extent I didn't know. I had never known anyone with an artificial leg. I had also never even seen anyone with one of these things on. An older man had come to demonstrate his below the knee artificial leg. He tap danced and even jumped over a chair.

That was nice to see, but I had never tap danced with my two legs and certainly had no desire to jump over chairs. He also had his knee joint. That makes all the difference in the world in a leg amputation. In fact on the ward knee joints were referred to as a "Million Dollar" knee joint. I just wanted to know how I could get from here to there and do everyday things! (This is the reason I wrote this book.)

The end of my stump healed over in less than a week. The doctor was surprised, but I said, "Remember? I told you that I healed fast." The next day when he made his rounds he asked me why I was still in bed.

I told him, "Every time I try to get up my back splits open!"

He said, "What!"

I answered, "Yes, my back opens up. It's that shrapnel wound!"

He grabbed my chart and shuffled down to one of the last pages. He looked at a page for a minute, shook his head and told me to roll over. This I did and he removed the old bandage, swabbed the wound with alcohol and with an "Ah-ha" and tweezers pulled something out of my back. Having visions of a nice metal fragment that would make me a great souvenir, I asked if I could have it. He said yes in a funny way and handed it to me. Alas, no souvenir! It was only a rather sickly looking wax draining plug.

The doctor then said, "Hang on. I'm going to cauterize it." Out of a small bottle he got a piece of sodium and dropped it on the wound. Luckily, the two large corpsmen that were with him grabbed me or I would have surely hit the ceiling. Boy! Did it hurt, but it was soon over and I would now be able to get out of bed.

That afternoon I asked our ward man for a pair of crutches. Our ward like the other orthopedic wards had two crutches and one wheelchair to be shared by 40 plus patients. I was lucky and did not have to wait. As I stuck the tops into my armpits and started for the men's room, I discovered that I had never used crutches before. However, after a few wobbly steps I got the hang of walking with them.

In the latrine I came to the conclusion that if it had to be, I could make it through life on crutches. After I relieved myself, I went over to wash my hands. I looked up and did not recognize the dirty, frowzy thin guy I was staring at. I looked terrible! I had lost a lot of weight even before I was wounded. One does not get fat eating "K" rations.

That plus being always on the go with usually not more than three hours sleep had reduced my 168 pounds, before combat, to I don't know what, but I looked like a walking dead man. I washed my hands and face. They were not so bad as a nurse, or me, had done that every morning in my hospital bed. What I needed was a bath and a shampoo.

I began to feel weak and woozy. It was the first time out of bed in about a month. I said to myself, "I'll do that the first thing tomorrow!" And I did. After seeing myself in the mirror, I was glad that I had not been sent directly home. One look at me and Mom would have passed out. With another month at my Oxford home I gained most of my weight back and finally got the last of combat dirt and blood off of me.

I spent another month in that hospital waiting, I thought, for an airlift back to the good ole U.S.A. One day two men showed up at my bedside pushing a cart with buckets and bags of what turned out to be plaster on it. They announced that they had come to put a traction shipping cast on me. I said what for. My stump has been healed over for at least a month.

That didn't faze them at all. It seems that army regulation required that I have this "traction cast," and there were no exceptions. Even the fact that I didn't need it made no difference! They began mixing the plaster in the buckets and wrapping me in gaze. When they had finished I had a cast on me that not only covered my stump but also came up and circled my waist. There was a heavy wire loop coming from the bottom of the cast sticking down about 18 inches. It had a little notch in the end that normally would have anchored a heavy elastic band that would have been attached to the slip sock that covered my stump.

# Chapter Three

## My First Try on an Artificial Leg

My stump was all healed and toughened up, but I was still waiting for my leg. Now I was not sitting round the hospital moping while I waited. I made full use of my crutches, going home for dinner every night and then out on the town. This was usually to Eddy's Friendly Tavern, a local beer joint in my neighborhood. However, I was still frustrated. I wanted to walk on two legs again!

At the "Glen" the wards consisted of several rooms with about five or six patients in each room. Before the army bought the girls school I guess these rooms would have been classrooms. One of the guys in my room had an old peg leg he was no longer using. It had been shoved under my bed.

This was a special kind of leg used to work the stiffness out of a knee joint. Often on a below the knee amputee this joint would stiffen from lack of use while the patient was confined to bed. It had a swivel platform where the knee rested while walking. The weight of the body during walking would gradually get the bend back in the knee. It had worked well for my fellow patient and he was now walking very well on the regular BK leg.

One afternoon while he was away at physical therapy I pulled it from under his bed and gave it a good once over. I stuck my stump in it and since I had my entire femur bone it almost fit. I figured if I stabilized the tilting platform at horizontal and put about three inches of padding in I could walk on it.

Bill came back from physical therapy and asked me if I was ready to go to lunch. I told him my idea about me and his leg. He said, "Sure, go ahead and use it. I don't want it anymore." When I got back from lunch I went to work on the leg and in no time had it fitting ok and strapped on around my waist. It felt fine, but the big question was, how would it walk for me?

I turned and faced the door to my room. Then I stepped out with the peg leg and let it hit the floor a foot or so in front of me, whatever was in easy reach. That worked ok so I stepped forward with my good leg. That worked fine too. I repeated these moves and I was walking. What a great feeling to be able to move along the hallway with my hands free and not gripping crutches.

In just a few minutes I was cruising along at a pretty good clip. I almost tripped once when I did not swing the leg out far enough, but I caught myself and made sure it didn't happen again. I walked to the big full-length mirror at the end of the hall to take a look at myself.

It was good to see me standing there without crutches. If I felt this good with this old makeshift leg, I wondered how good I would feel with a new leg made just for me. I turned to do some more walking and one of my fellow amputee patients said, "Hi! You're looking good, but don't let the nurse or doctor catch you!"

I wondered why. I thought they would be pleased to see me walking. However, I was wrong and my friend was correct. I was about half way back to my room when the head nurse came roaring up to me shouting some unlady like army phrases and telling me to get the leg off and to keep it off. She was a Captain and I was a PFC, so I said 'Yes, Ma'm and did what she said.

It seems like they thought by using a peg leg I would develop bad walking habits. Like throwing it to the side causing a limping action in my walking. Maybe it would, she and the doctor had a lot more experience with artificial legs than I did, but I felt that I could have adjusted my manner of walking to a regular prosthesis.

I think that episode might have helped the Doc to realize that I was ready for my leg. He was a very good doctor and knew what being an amputee was all about as he had lost his right leg below the knee some time ago and had enlisted in the army to help us guys with the knowledge he had gained not only in medical school, but also as a fellow amputee. He also had had a bad time with a poor surgical job.

# Chapter Four

## I Finally Get My Prosthesis

The day came when I received my orders to go to the limb shop to be fitted for my new genuine official army issue artificial leg. The limb shop was in the main section so I hurried to the shuttle bus stop as fast as my crutches would carry me. By now I could travel at a pretty good clip on them.

Once in the limb shop a technician measured my stump in every direction possible. He also measured the length of my good leg and the distance around my calf. He then went over to a wall that was lined from floor to ceiling with rows of what looked like over sized milk bottles. He selected one and brought it back and held it next to my good lower leg.

After writing my name on it he explained that the "milk bottle" was to be my lower leg. He kind of laughed and said, "It's not pretty, but it does the job for a temporary training leg. There is no reason to waste a lot of money on a fancy looking leg that you will only wear for about four months. When your stump hardens to the job and takes on its more or less permanent shape, you will be able to go to civilian leg maker and get a more realistic looking one."

At this point I didn't care how it looked, only how it worked. I went back to Forest Glen Rehab Center to wait for them to make my new GI leg. I first met my new leg a week later in walking class. My doctor was there to check its fit and I guess me too. This was the first time I met the 100 percent virgin wool stump sock that was to become part of my wardrobe for the rest of my life. Except for the years I wore a suction socket leg.

The good doctor was pleased with everything so the PT tech helped me over to the parallel railings designed to help those learning to walk again either with artificial legs or their own. They reminded me of the parallel bars in my high school gym class. I was so elated that I felt like doing a handstand on them like I did back then.

I resisted the urge and turned my attention to what my instructor was saying. It went something like this, "Kick the leg out firmly, but gentle. You don't want your step to look jerky." This I did according to instructions stepped through with my real leg. It was a little jerky, but not bad for my first steps. By the time I reached the end of the railings I had the knack of it and walked right out into the room.

The instructor noted that I had good balance coordination so he told me to go on back to my ward, but to return the next day. He also told me to work on smoothing out my gait. This I did. My hip joint began to feel sore and I discovered some muscles in my stump that had not been used for many months. However, the experience of walking again on two legs overshadowed any soreness.

The next day I reported for more practice at the class and did more walking around the hospital. This same day the Public Information Officer for the Medical Center called on me. He told me now that the war was over they were starting a new bond drive. A Victory Bond Drive instead of the War Bonds that I had helped to sell many times before.

He would like me to go to Richmond, Virginia and speak to all of the schools and maybe a factory or two. I was to point out that although the war was over money was still needed for the wounded still hospitalized and to help rehabilitate them. I could use myself as an example. Yes, they would give me facts and figures to use in my talks.

I was a little afraid of undertaking this trip with only two days on my leg. There might be a lot of walking but I could leave my leg back at the hospital and go on my crutches as I had on speaking engagements in the past. I didn't want to do that! It would seem to me like a set back. I decided to go with my new leg.

It was a good decision. Walking the streets of Richmond turned out to be a better teacher than any school could be. Once out of the door in the morning there was no turning back to get my crutches. There was no stopping if I got a little tired. I just dug down for some extra strength and continued on. My combat experience helped me with this, as an infantryman was always working tired and digging down!

I did use a cane during these early days of "walking again". It helped me if I got a little tired, but most of all it let the other pedestrians know I had a handicap. Even so I often got "run over" in a rushing crowd. It was also a good weapon, but I am glad to say I never had to use it as such. It also helped with hailing a cab.

The first time I crossed a street in downtown Richmond the curb on the other side looked a mile high. I wondered how I would ever get up it. When I go there it wasn't the mountain it seemed at a distance and with a little extra ooff on the cane I was on the sidewalk again. Each time I did a curb they became easier until I no longer thought about them.

One day my speaking assignments ended a little after noon. My transportation was taking me back to the house in the suburbs where I had a room. It was a hot day and a hot day in Richmond, like any river "town", was also very humid. I decided I did not want to go back to the house. The people who owned it were very nice, but there was nothing to do. I asked the driver to let me off. I wanted a cold beer.

I was still in downtown Richmond. I looked all around and walked a block or two. Not a sign of any tavern. I saw a drugstore sign at the end of a long block. I wondered if I could walk that far. I was about to chicken out and call a cab for "home" when I decided I could make it. I estimated that the distance was about three times the distance from my ward to the restroom and I knew I could walk that.

I started out for the sign at the end of the block. My calculations had not taken into account that the sidewalk had a bit of an upgrade and it was a very humid 90 degrees. Near the end I had to dig down for some reserve infantry strength, but I made it. I sat down on a stool at the soda fountain and ordered an ice tea with lemon. It looked great until the guy next to me ordered a frosty mug of beer.

During all this walking I discovered a new way of doing it. I found that if I stepped out with my good foot, or leg, I could then let my artificial leg just swing through and when the knee was straight again step down on it. This eliminated the kicking motion that was a "trademark" of an above the knee artificial leg. One had to be careful that the sole of the shoe was high enough to clear the ground.

# Chapter Five

## I Volunteer to Sell V-Bonds

I had been at Walter Reed for about four months and now my artificial leg felt like it was part of me and I was walking very well. I had crossed that invisible line where I would rather go to "town" or any place with my leg instead of my crutches. During the first weeks of getting use to it and walking, it was all done around the hospital during the day. When it came time to go to town and Eddy's Friendly Tavern, the leg went under my bed and out came my crutches.

I don't know exactly when I crossed this line, but one evening one of my ward mates said to me, "Hey! You've crossed the line!" I asked him what line was he talking about and he explained that I was wearing my leg into town, or whatever, in preference to my crutches. We both agreed that I was rehabilitated as well as I was going to get here in the hospital.

This meant discharge time was nearing and I would return to civilian life and college. I hadn't thought much about it as I went

Horsing around with my new Army issue prosthesis. It was great to be walking again on two legs. Here I am sitting on the back steps at my home haming it up for the camera.

WoW! Here I am all duded up as a civilian. I can't remember where I was going. Looks like maybe to some one's wedding. It took a while to get use to the loose fit of the non GI clothes, but here I look at ease with my civies.

# Chapter Six

## And Now Back to College

One of the first things on my list to do as I entered civilian life was to get back to college. If it had not been for the war and losing my leg, I would have gone to Duke University in North Carolina. I liked the school and the campus. There was also a good friend of the family who had graduated from there and was eager to recruit me, so to speak, for his alma mater.

I had been assured that my track record in high school would qualify me for a scholarship. Of course there would be no more track competition for me. I had decided while I was still in the hospital that I did not want to go that far away from home for two reasons. One being that I had been away for almost three years and the other was my artificial leg.

I could have gone back to George Washington University. It was close to home, but I did not like the set up there for classes. It was a city college that catered to part time students, many from the federal government. This meant classes running into the night. The quality of education was very good, but I wanted a bit more of a campus as well as a more compact class schedule.

Due to the "G.I. Bill" money was not a problem. My Mother and Father had saved money for my college education and I had also put money away for this event. Now I would get my education paid for by Public Law 16. This was like the G.I. Bill, but was for rehabilitating war wounded and was considered part of their rehab.

Looking over the field of Universities not too far away from home, I decided that Western Maryland would be a nice place to go. It was a small college to the west of Washington, D.C. in the foothills of the Blue Ridge Mountains. It also seemed to have a nice personality.

I wrote them and set up an appointment for an interview with the dean of admissions. My Father took a day off from work and drove me out there. When we arrived at the campus it was everything I had expected. It looked like a University perhaps out of a Hollywood movie. I scanned the campus and noted the buildings. They were fairly close together and the land was flat enough for my artificial leg and me to get around.

I was dressed in my civilian best and Dad looked great in his business suit. Like the top lawyer he was. We met the dean with a lot of shaking of hands and smiling faces. The dean gave me his PR talk about the history and accomplishments of his school. I asked him about the pre-med courses. They had a two-year one and a three-year one. Both accepted by the University of Maryland Medical School in Baltimore. In fact Western Maryland was part of the University of Maryland.

All was great so far. Then I mentioned that I had been wounded in combat during defense of Bastogne during the Battle of the Bulge and had an artificial leg. Would I be able to use my car (yet to come) around the campus? The answer surprised me. It was, "No! Students are not allowed to have cars. There are no exceptions!"

Wow! That was a shock, but what he said to me next was worse. He told my Dad and I that they didn't really want veterans on their nice little campus. They were loud, noisy and drank too much. He added that they were also "womanizers". Wow! Again. Another example of patriotism going down the drain at war's end.

I was glad my Father was there for I'm sure if he had not been I would have hit him in the nose right then and there. He backed off a bit and said that I did not look like I'd be troublesome on the campus and he could not refuse me admission if I chose to enroll.

I stood up. My Dad stood up. I said back to him that he need not worry. I would not consider going to any University with such an attitude and policy. Then we both walked out of the door without saying goodbye. Out in the car on the way back home Dad congratulated me on my stand.

The next day I wrote a letter to the University of Maryland in College Park, Maryland. I included my transcript from high school and George Washington. It probably was longer, but it seemed like the next day I got my acceptance and instructions about what to do and who to see on registration day.

I should add here that the University of Maryland had not been my first choice as back in the twenties and thirties when I was growing up it was considered an agriculture college and not much more. However, one look at the campus told my Father and I that that was no longer true.

THE BLUE BULLET- This is my 1946 model 76 Oldsmobile. My Mother called it the "Blue Bullet," I hope for its nice light blue color and streamlined back and not my driving style although it was a very "Peppy" car.

It was a gloriously large campus. I wondered how I would be able to cover all of this territory.

My Father dropped me off in front of a red brick building that had a big sign hanging on it saying, "Register Here." I went up the long flight of stairs and was glad I had my cane with me. At the door a young lady with some kind of armband on greeted me. I showed her the letter I had received and she led me over to a special table.

What a difference from that other college. Every one had a friendly greeting and I, as a wounded veteran, was given VIP treatment. I had no trouble setting up a limited schedule. There was even a representative from the Veterans Administration who helped me with the pile of forms, etc. to be filled out for Public Law 16.

I had been so busy that I almost forgot to ask about my use of a car. I was told to wait where I was. The word was passed along and a tall broad shouldered policeman soon arrived at my table. He introduced himself as "Dan Wiseman, Chief of the University Police Force". I told him my problems with my artificial leg. He disappeared and returned with a rather large red window sticker.

He handed it to me and said, "You can park anyplace on the campus except by a fireplug or blocking a loading platform." He added that if I had any problems to just give him a call and he handed me his business card. The Chief walked me out of the door and down the steps.

There sitting under the shade tree enjoying the view was my Father. I introduced him to Chief Wiseman and Dad went to get the car. On the way home we stopped at the University Bookstore and I got what was necessary for my three courses including paper, pencils and a pen. I looked at the tab and thanked my government for picking up the bill.

It was great to be back at the books again, but I found it hard to sit still during long periods of study. It looks like here I must be writing "an award winning" article for the university newspaper.

# Chapter Seven

## The Ocean and Me: Two Legs and One

From age six on, my first vacation at Rehoboth Beach, Delaware, I spent my summer vacations on the sandy beaches of this ocean resort swimming among and diving through salty waves. I became a pretty good surf swimmer and learned how to handle the largest curlers by diving straight through them.

I felt at home in the waves and would often float on my back just beyond their breaking point for a half hour or more. However, the ocean's waves are not a place to learn how to be a good swimmer. I had my style of dog paddle, but nothing that even came close to resembling Johnny Wiesmuler and the Australian crawl.

The summer of 1945 found me at Walter Reed Army hospital after losing my right leg in combat. My Mom and Dad asked me if I would like to go to Rehoboth again for vacation. Boy, it sounded great to me, but I told them that I would have to check with my doctor and get leave from the army.

I was still on crutches waiting for my stump to get ready for an artificial leg. When I asked the doctor, Major DeSantis, he said, "Why sure you can go. In fact the sun and salt water would do your stump good." He furnished a statement to that effect and the personnel guys gave me a two-week pass. I had not had any official leave since I had returned to the States as I lived almost in the medical centers backyard.

So once again the three of us were off for the beach. It had been three years since our last visit to Rehoboth and things were different now. I worried a little as to how I'd get along on the beach and in the water with only one leg and on crutches. However, I knew I would still enjoy the beach and sun. I was also determined to go swimming in the surf.

We set up our umbrella near the lifeguard stand and close to the water, but not too close. I hopped around to get my beach towel laid out nice and flat in the sun near the umbrellas. Dad laid his towel in the sun also. The umbrella was for Mother as she had fair skin and it burned very easily.

I picked up my crutches, they were the conventional wooden kind, and headed for the water. Near the water's edge I hit a soft spot in the wet sand and my right crutch sank a foot down into it. I almost went over on my nose, but didn't. I yanked my crutch out, found a firm section of beach and headed into the water. I had just learned one of the hazards of using crutches on the beach.

I walked out until the water was over my ankles. Whoops! Ankle! I was standing there enjoying the feel of the cold ocean water sloshing over my foot with each incoming wave. I was wondering how much more I could penetrate this majestic body of water when Dad appeared at my elbow. He said, "Let's go out a little more and get our suits wet. I'll be right here in case you need me."

When we got out to where the water was up to our waists, I thought, "What the hell!"

This was a dangerous spot. The place in the surf where a wave could really whack you one. I handed Dad my crutches and dove into the next wave. Hey! It was great. Just like before I lost my leg. In fact, it was better. I was more buoyant.

I paddled out past the breaking point of the waves, rolled over into a back float and waved to Dad still standing in the surf holding my crutches. I told him I was fine and that I would give him a wave when I wanted to come in. I lay there floating around, but being careful not to drift out to sea.

It was like I was whole again, but with only half the kicking power. That didn't matter too much for as I said before I was no great swimmer. What I lost in kicking power, I made up for with my arms. I don't know what kind of stroke it was, but my two good arms could propel me through the seawater and waves at a pretty good pace.

When I was ready to come in I waved and Dad got off his blanket in the sun and waded in to meet me with my crutches in his hand. I picked a nice "round" wave and rode it in. I ended up right at my Father's side. He helped me up and I grabbed my crutches and we walked out of the ocean and back to our beach towels together with me just babbling away as to how great it was.

I lay down on my towel face up to enjoy the feeling of the warm sun evaporating the seawater from my skin leaving little salt crystals. My Mother said that the lifeguard almost fell off of his stand when he saw me coming out of the water on crutches. Mom said that he had not noticed me when I went in for my swim with Dad at my side.

I went over to the lifeguard and introduced myself and told him that I was sorry to have startled him. He said, "That's ok. It was the first time I had ever seen a one legged man on crutches coming out of the ocean." I guess it did look rather unusual, but the lifeguards at Rehoboth soon got used to me.

When my vacation was over and I returned to the hospital, my doctor was very pleased with what he saw. I was brown as a berry. (That's what my Mother used to say about me when I had collected a good suntan. I don't know where she got the expression as I have never seen a "brown berry," at least I do not recall seeing a berry of brown.) The sun and salt water had put the finishing touches on my stump. The scar from the operation was well healed and my naturally tough hide even tougher. I was ready for my leg!

ENJOYING THE SUN at Rehoboth Beach, Del. with son and lady friend. The sun and salt water helped to keep the skin on my stump in good condition.

said, "What's the matter? Ain't you ever seen any one who lost a leg in the war?"

Now they felt uncomfortable and I somewhat relieved. One thing I was sure of was that I was not going to let some rude person interfere with what I wanted to do. If I was asked a question in a decent fashion about my leg or lack of it, I was not offended. I answered any question that was asked of me.

I had a good friend, Charlie Kutovicz, he felt different about his wounds. Charlie had been with the Third Infantry Division in Italy. He had first been wounded when a needle like piece of shell fragment hit him in one cheek and came out of the other. It left him with two natural looking dimples. However, that small piece of metal had taken out his front teeth.

They sent him back to his outfit and combat as soon as the flesh wounds healed. But without any false choppers. Charlie always bitched about that. I would kid him back with "What the hell did you want to do? Chew the enemy to death?" He would say that that was not the point, there was an army regulation requiring soldiers to have teeth before going into combat.

He also, on this second trip to the front, stepped on a "shoe-mine". This is a small all-plastic mine about the size of a shoebox. It was designed to blow ones foot off somewhere above the ankle. That's what this one did to Charlie. His leg was gone right at the calf.

Charlie would not go to town or even come to my house for dinner. He said, "I'm staying right here in the hospital until the army gives me a leg and some teeth." I told him that was too bad.

He was missing some good times and headed out the hospital gate on my crutches. Now Charlie was far from being anti-social and when he got his leg and teeth he sure made up for lost time. I will add here that he walked on that below the knee leg without the slightest limp.

# Chapter Nine

## An Experience That Charlie Missed

One bright sunny afternoon I had just returned from a swim in the ocean and had stretched out on my back to dry off in the sun. I was lying there with my eyes closed and about half asleep. I got the feeling that someone was looking at me. I opened my eyes and there at the foot of my bath towel stood the cutest four-year old girl I had ever seen.

She was just standing there with a very worried expression on her young face. She asked me very politely what had happened to my leg. I asked her if she knew what war was. She replies, "Yes. I've seen it in the movies." I explained that I had been one of those men firing guns at our enemy.

I continued telling her that the enemy fired their guns at us in return. Some of their bullets hit my leg and it was so broken up that even the best doctors could not fix it. They had to remove the broken part. She just stood there not saying a word but taking in everything that I said.

In a second or two after I had finished she broke her silence. "Does it hurt?" she asked.

"No!" I told her.

She replied, "Oh! I'm so glad!" and turned and went back to her parents snoozing under their beach umbrella.

That was one of the most heart-warming experiences of my life. Children have a natural curiosity. It is how they learn things, by asking questions. If they are polite, and most of them have been, I always answer their questions. I always try to find out what they know about war and if they have seen it in the movies or on television and tie my experience into theirs.

Of course I do not go into any of the gory details, but make it simply like my response to the little lady on the beach. The parents often get embarrassed and try to pull their child away. When I can, I tell them not to worry. I didn't mind the questions. I usually end by telling the youngster to be careful on their bike and watch out for traffic, as these are also ways one could get hurt and lose a leg.

THE BACKSIDE of my son , Dad and I fishing at Indian River Inlet, Del .
We didn 't cath catch much but had a lot of sun and fun.

seemed, although the bus service covered a vast area, it did not go close enough to where I wanted to go most of the time. I was also planning to attend the University of Maryland and there was not adequate bus service to and from there.

I had enough money to buy a new car. In fact I had ordered one from my Father's Oldsmobile Dealer soon after I arrived at the hospital. This had been before civilian car production had begun. I should add here that at this time there were only two makes of automobiles manufactured that had a fully automatic transmission. They were Cadillac and Oldsmobile. The Caddies were definitely above the family and my budget.

However, the Oldsmobile was within my price range. Especially the smaller six cylinder models. Dad had driven an Oldsmobile since 1936 and now had an almost new 1941 Ninety-Eight four-door sedan. It was a great car and I had driven it often before the war, but it did not have the "hydromatic drive" so was useless to me now.

When Mr. Mann of Mann's Oldsmobile visited me in the hospital as a family friend, I had ordered a fastback two door, six-cylinder sedan. He had put me at the top of his waiting list so I thought I was all set. This feeling was reinforced when my car arrived before I was discharged and well before I had enrolled in any college. It was a grand looking car in one of my favorite shades of blue.

My Mother called it "The Blue bullet" because of its streamlined back. (Not my driving I hope.) This was great. This was wonderful; except for the fact that Mr. Mann could not sell it to me. The Federal Government had to decide some kind of tax or fee to be set on the new post war cars. It took them well over six months to make up their mind. Meanwhile my car sat there in the dealer's showroom all bright and beautiful and I had no transportation.

When I enrolled at Maryland for the spring session I did not take on a full schedule. It had been over three years since I had sat in a classroom at George Washington University and I knew my brain was rusty. This also gave me some leeway in arranging classes that would give me time to get from one class to another.

My first month of getting to college and around the campus was quite a task. Thanks to friends I did not miss any classes. My car still sat at the dealer as the government was still trying to make up their mind. I noticed that Ford had more cars on the street than any other manufacturer. I had also read in the newspaper about a "Victory Kit" for disabled veterans that would allow an above the knee amputee to drive a standard tranny.

That sounded good so I took a chance and wrote a letter to the Ford Company explaining my situation including the car still confined to the dealer. In a short length of time I received a form letter explaining their long waiting list for wantabe car buyers. They stated that they were sorry, "but they could not help me!" I tossed it aside and forgot all about it. A shot in the dark that had missed.

About a week later when I got home from school at about 2pm, there was a note that Mom had left on the dining room table telling me to call Hill and Tibbets. This was a Ford dealer in downtown Washington, D.C. I had never been there. I dialed the number and waited. A nice female voice said hello and asked whom I wanted to speak to. I told her I was returning a call from someone there, but didn't have the name. A Mr. Saunders came on the phone and asked if I was Don Addor of 1428 Geranium Street. I said yes. He said that they had a new car for me. To myself I said, "Wow!"

I asked him when I could get it and how much money would I need. He said, "Anytime and about $980. I told him I would call back, hung up and dialed my Father at his office downtown. I told him about the car and money needed. He said he could make the bank before it closed and would meet me at the dealership in an hour. After a long wait things were really happening fast. I had the money for the car in my savings account, but I would not have been able to get it until the next day. Dad worked at the Internal Revenue Building, just a short walk from his bank.

I tried to get myself organized and wrote a note to Mom telling her where I was going and why. I walked up to Alaska Avenue just in time to catch a bus. Down 16th Street we went and made pretty good time, as there were not many travelers at this time of day. All of this time I was wondering how this had happened. Who pulled the string that produced this car? I couldn't figure it out, but I knew a lot of friends and family had been trying to locate one for me. I had forgotten all about that form letter from the Ford Company as it had been a T.S. slip of the first order, or so it seemed.

I got off the bus at K Street and made the short walk to Hill and Tibbets. My Father and Mr. Saunders were there waiting for me. It seemed that Dad and Mr. Saunders had met years ago when Mr. Saunders was a young salesman and Dad purchased his first car from him, a Model-T. Mr. Saunders took us to the service department and pointed to a beautiful metallic gray, two-door sedan. The men were still getting it cleaned and ready after its long trip from the factory. "Man! Was it a beaut!"

We went back and did the paper work. I signed on the bottom line and the car was mine. Mr. Saunders showed me the "Victory Kit." It was a vacuum activated clutch and would be installed tomorrow. I could pick up the car then with its temporary tags and registration. That was it. All was done, but before we left I asked Mr. Saunders how come the car and me. I added that he knew we had never been to his dealership. He said it came in from the factory this morning with my name and address on it. It was in addition to their quota. He looked up the telephone number and called. That's all he knew.

I told him about the letter I had written and the "form letter" answer just a week ago. He said that had to be it. I went home and sat right down and wrote Mr. Ford a very nice "Thank you" letter. I never heard anymore from the Ford Company. I sure hope they got my letter. I had wheels again, well almost. I still had to go to the D.C. Motor Vehicle Department and get tags on it and I would have to get a new driver's license. My D.C. permit had expired while I was in the service and my army one was no good for a civilian. I wasn't looking forward to it either, but it had to be done. This was a big part of becoming a civilian again and the beginning of life as a one legged man in a two legged world.

My new Ford car was great, but the "Victory Kit", a vacuum operated clutch, was something else. It was either in or out. Ideal for a dragster, but not so good in traffic. I checked, but there was no way to adjust its speed in and out. I soon got used to it and all went well. The biggest problem was reverse. This being a low ratio gear, when the clutch flew out the car shot back like a cannon ball.

I practiced for a day or two on the tempo dealer tags, and then headed across town to Washington, D.C. traffic department for my regular tags and a new driver's permit. When I arrived there everyone was very helpful and I got all the paper work done and my new license plates in no time. The hitch on the permit was that I would have to take a driving test to see if a one-legged man with a special clutch could drive a car safely. Mine was the first "Victory Kit" that they had seen.

The driving test was given on the city's streets, not a course marked out on a parking lot. We got my car. I got behind the wheel and the officer rode next to me in the passenger's seat. I had good luck and that ole vacuum clutch worked like a charm. Then came the request to parallel park. This meant the dreaded backing up. I was glad that I had practiced this. The officer pointed to an empty parking spot in front of the building and said, "Park there". I had hoped for a couple of poles to back in, but this was for real.

I did some calculations in my head and pulled up parallel about three cars in front of the opening. Now the usual distance is about half a car. The officer asked me what I was doing way down the street. I told him that the clutch was a little tricky in reverse. He said, "Oh" and gave me a funny look. Into reverse I went. The clutch came flying out and back I went. I'm not sure if the tires actually burned rubber, but it was close to it. I heard the officer suck in his breath as I flew back. Then a quick right and left and then stand on the brakes.

I had made a perfect parking job. Just the correct distance from the curb and the cars in front and back.

The officer wiped his brow, went to his clipboard and did some writing. He handed me the paper. I had passed. He got out of the car and wished me lots of luck and mumbled that he would not go near a car like that again for all the tea in China. I don't think he heard me, but as he walked away I told him that I did not plan to do much, if any, parallel parking. The Ford was a very nice car and sure helped to get from here to there, but I was glad when in a couple of months my Oldsmobile with its smooth driving hydromatic was delivered.

As soon as I received the Ford I had written to Mr. Ford thanking him. I also promised when and if I sold the car, it would be to an amputee war veteran. I don't know if he ever saw my letter or not, but apparently he saw my first letter – a request for help.

I stayed true to my promise and when my Olds with hydromatic was finally mine I put notice on the bulletin boards in the amputee wards at nearby Walter Reed. The price was just what I paid for it, something just under $1,000. The ad specified "For Sale to an Amputee", but most, who showed up, although from Walter Reed Hospital, were not even patients.

My Mother had to deal with most of those eager to have a new 1946 car as I was usually away at school when they knocked on the door of 1428 Geranium Street. Mother would just tell them no, they didn't qualify. Most understood the term necessary requirement, so after a try said goodbye. There was one young Lieutenant who was very persistent. When Mother said he didn't qualify, me misunderstood and pulled out a big roll of bills and said, "Just name your price!" Mother just shook her head and the confused young officer went away wondering why he had failed. The reason for all of these eager people with eyes on my car was because there was still a long waiting list, at least six months, for new cars from a dealer.

A lot of potential sales with the opportunity to make a few hundred dollars profit, came and went. I checked the wards again to find that most of the combat wounded amputees had been discharged and gone home. I was about to give up my promise as unable to keep when I got a call from a young man asking if I still had the car. I said yes. He said yes, he was an amputee. I told him the car was his. The next day he came to the house with cash that had been wired to him from his home. He counted it out on our dining room table, all $980 of it. He sat down and with a sigh said, "That is the most money I have ever seen in my life."

We finished signing over the title and he drove it while I explained the workings of the "funny clutch". He got the knack of it right away. He told me he was being discharged the next day and would be driving home to the Pittsburgh, Pennsylvania area. The big smile on his face as he pulled away from my home was all the extra compensation I wanted or needed. I was glad I had stuck to my promise. Now another war amputee had Mr. Ford's car.

Oh, yes, about two years later I received a letter in the mail. It was from the buyer of that car thanking me and telling me how many miles it had helped him.

# Chapter Twelve

## A Lucky Break - Shoe Wise

One day back in about 1948, I got a real deal on a pair of shoes thanks to my artificial leg, or rather foot. I never was one for high class, big name shoes. Instead I bought middle priced shoes from a national chain store. The one that I had found that suited me best in my area, Silver Spring, Maryland, was Hanover. There were two reasons that I looked for the lower priced shoes. One was, it did not make me feel as bad when the toe of the shoe on my "wooden" foot got caught on something and got scratched. The other was the budget of a college student.

When I found a style of shoe that I liked, I stayed with it, if I could. Today I was after a new pair of shoes as the one on my left foot, the real one, was almost worn through. I could feel a grain of sand when I stepped on one. The shoe on my real foot was the one that always wore out, usually the sole. The one on the other foot was still almost like new except for a few scratches on the toe that could be rubbed down so as to be almost invisible. Also due to the lack of body oil and sweat in that foot the color tone on the shoe was almost the same as when it was purchased.

It was a nice sunny day as I approached the Hanover Shoe store on lower Georgia Avenue. I stopped and looked at the shoes in the window and saw the one I wanted. They were just like the good old ones I was now wearing. I entered the store and was greeted by a salesman who I had not met before. After the usual greeting and a comment on the nice weather, he asked me what I would like. I said a pair of shoes like the ones I was standing in. He took a glance down and then tried to interest me in a more expensive and more stylish pair. I sat down and he brought me a shoe that was very nice with a beautiful shiny toe. He said they were on sale.

I looked at it and saw that in addition to the smooth toes that would show scratches, it had leather soles and leather heels. I told him no. I needed leather soles, but rubber heels. A leather heel on the artificial foot on a hard surface would send me scooting across the room. That's why I wanted a shoe like I'm wearing. He sat on his stool and started to take the shoe off of my right foot. This is the custom in the shoe trade. Fit the right foot and the left will be ok. He got a funny expression on his face when he felt my artificial ankle.

I told him to fit my real foot. My left foot. He checked the number inside my shoe and went back to the stockroom. He was gone for a while and when he came back he said that he was sorry, but they were out of this model in my size. I told him there was a pair in the window. Could I buy those? He said sure and went and got them. I was in luck, they were my size – at least the left one was. The fit was perfect. The salesman looked at the right one and told me it was a size smaller. A pair had gotten mixed up somewhere, somehow.

He said he was really sorry. I told him not to worry, as my artificial foot was not the same size as my good one. I suggested that we try it on to see if the smaller shoe would fit. While he was pulling the old one off I laughed and said, "I could always sand the foot down to fit the shoe." We had a good laugh over my comment. However, with just a little extra effort the shoe went right on. "Good", I said, "I will take them. No! No box. I'll wear them home and you can throw the others away for me." At the cash register he said, "I can't charge full price for a mismatched pair of shoes. I'll give you 50% off as faulty merchandise."

That made me happy. A new pair of shoes for half price due to my "wooden" foot. Before I walked out the door he said, half to me and half to himself, "I wonder what customer is walking about out there with the other pair of different sized shoes?"

involving dirt and/or sand. Just a little bit of this stuff getting inside my sock would grind those pieces of rubber away. I also broke one of these ankles when lifting weights.

This new ankle, called the Sacht foot, was made up of a group of tough sponge material layered and sealed together in such a way that it gave near normal ankle movement. This worked great for walking and there was no way for dirt and sand to get inside and destroy the parts. There were no parts. After this new ankle had been attached to my leg I was briefed on how it worked and some of its limitations. I then went back to school and continued doing all of the things I did. The ankle worked great. Better than the old one with less worry about dirt, sand and water getting in it. I was truly satisfied and pleased with this new development.

After several months I was called back to appear before the Orthopedic Board and make a report on how the ankle worked in "real life." I made my report and every one was pleased and the "Sacht Foot" was accepted. As I was about to leave, they looked more closely at my feet and commented, "We forgot to tell you that you can't walk in those kind of shoes!" I was wearing what was called back then "penny loafers", a kind of slip on shoe with no laces or straps. They got their name from a piece of leather trim across the top front that had a little slit or pocket in it. In this slit, one put a shinny new penny. They often came with pennies in them.

I told the Doc that I had had no trouble walking in them and no they didn't tend to slip off. They were fine. I added that I was glad that they forgot to tell me I couldn't walk with a loafer type shoe, as I would have wasted a perfectly good pair of new shoes.

The members of the board gathered around took a closer look and made some new notations. One of them asked me what I had in the slits, as they were not the usual copper pennies. I popped one out and showed him. They were a penny-sized coin I had gotten in the hospital in England. They were three pences, a British coin of brass with squared off sides like an octagon only more so. This type of foot went on to serve the amputee (leg) well for many years.

The next item the Orthopedic Board called me about was a new type of leg with a suction socket. This meant the leg would be held on the body; stump, by suction and not by the big leather belt that went around one's waist. There would be a lightweight belt to act as a safety "chain" should anything happen to the suction power.

Boy! Did that sound great. The most uncomfortable thing for me about wearing an artificial leg was that belt under my clothes. In hot weather it was a double mess. I sweat a lot and that belt would get very wet with my sweat. Not only did it feel uncomfortable, but also on long hot days the leather did not smell too good.

They explained to me that the leg had been tested on a couple of amputees with ideal stumps, an ideal stump for an above the knee amputee being half way down the thigh bone and having no scar tissue, and it worked nicely for them. They knew that my AK stump was far from ideal as my leg had been cut through the knee joint leaving my entire femur bone.

This was an idea developed during World War II for an amputation that would let one walk on the femur bone with the leg held on by a kind of corset laced around the thigh and with no big belt around the waist. There were two types, an end bearing and a weight bearing. I don't remember which was which, but one had the kneecap turned under and adhered to the end of the femur bone. The other, like me, just had the femur bone end to take the weight.

This was good in theory but not so hot in practice. There was too much weight for the end of the bone to carry with comfort and the girdle did not hold it in place either. By the time I got my second leg, I had one with a full-length willow wood socket and a leather belt to hold it on. Now this sounded like a chance to get rid of that damn belt. The spokesman for the board explained to me, that after reviewing my file, they had decided that if they could make a suction socket work on my long skinny stump, they could make it work on anyone. That sounded a bit "iffy", but I sure would try to make it work.

I went to the Universal Artificial Limb Company, in downtown Washington, D.C. at that time, and they went to work to build me a suction socket leg. The first problem that came up had to do with my long stump and where my artificial knee joint would wind up. This would be a good bit lower than my real one on the left. On the leg I was using, my knee joint was a little lower, but the space needed for the suction would make it at least two inches lower. This looked a bit unusual when I was sitting down, but that didn't bother me. However, the Orthopedic Board questioned if I could walk properly with one knee lower than the other.

After all the measurements were taken and a plaster cast was made of my stump, Vic Caron and his workers at Universal went ahead and built me a fine leg held on by suction.

When the leg was finished the knee joint was a good bit lower than my real one, but on the plus side there was no thick heavy belt. On my first trial walking up and down the length of the limb shop, everything went fine. Actually that's an understatement – it was great! The lowered knee made no difference in my gait and the suction held my leg so firmly that there actually was no up and down movement inside the socket when I walked.

I would have liked to walk right home with it, but there was still more work to be done. Most of this cosmetic, like smoothing down the willow wood and giving it a coat or two of skin tone paint. I knew the orthopedic guy at The Pentagon would be pleased and so would many more amputees.

Another great thing about the suction socket was that there was no need for those heavy wool stump socks. Down at the bottom of the socket there was a valve that helped create the suctions. To get the leg on, one removed the valve and put a "slip sock" through the opening.

Then the stump went into the stump slip sock and you pulled the sock out through the hole as you entered the leg socket.

Then, one screwed in the valve and pushed down into the socket. Suction was created and the leg clung firmly to your stump. There was no hot stump sock. Only you and your skin against the smooth lacquered side of the socket. I never cared for doing laundry. To me it was one of the evil necessities of life and those ole stump socks of virgin wool took special treatment.

While we were planning the wedding the father suggested that perhaps it would be better for my artificial leg and me if Veronica and I were seated during the event. I guess he was afraid that I might fall down. I almost agreed, but suddenly remembered the noise my suction socket leg might make when I stood up. That would be a sure shocker!

I explained to Father Byrolli that when I sat down with this leg it lost the suction. In theory, when I stood back up and pressed down to restore suction the air should pass out a valve in the bottom of my leg making no more than a slight hiss. Hardly noticeable at all in a crowd.

In reality most of the air shot up the side of the socket and when it squeezed out at the top between me and my leg it sounded like an elephant passing gas, or in plain words, a great "fart" would resound through the church's hall and high ceiling.

Everyone agreed that that would all but ruin this solemn event. I would get married standing, vertical that is! I would not fall down. There could be no rehearsal, as the wedding party could not arrive before the day of the wedding. However, I was shown the path the groom was to take from behind the alter, past the podium and down a short, narrow flight of stairs to the main floor of the building.

I tried the route a couple of times and had no problems at all. Veronica rehearsed her part with stand ins. Her Uncle Joseph would give her away as her father had been dead for several years. Her Uncle Joseph lived in New Jersey and would arrive the morning of the nuptials. Her maid of honor, the friend of my best man, would also arrive from Washington, D.C. about an hour before.

There was no worry about Uncle Joseph. He was a very stylish Irishman who led the Tipperary Contingent every year in New York City's St. Patrick's Day Parade. All he had to do was to enter the arched doorway and strut down the center aisle with his niece on his arm.

For Oscar his part was little more complicated. Not only was Oscar my best man and had to lead me to the altar, but he was also the wedding singer and had to start the ceremony from high in the balcony where the organist sat at the keyboard. When he finished singing he had to run down the stairs, out the front door along the outside of the church and then in to a small side door and the rear of the stage or altar.

Oscar was my singer because he was one of the best country western artists in D.C. and Eastern Shore area. I was also the band's promotion man. It would be the first time my mother as well as many friends had heard Oscar sing.

I mailed a diagram and instructions to Oscar and he called me to say, "Not to worry! It was a piece of cake." I told him that I wished he had not used the term, "piece of cake." He asked "Why?" I told him to check back and he would see that most of his "pieces of cake" turned into trouble. He reassured me that everything would be fine and that he and Bonnie were looking forward to the wedding.

The day of the wedding came. It was a cold December day with the temperature around the freezing point. I rubbed my stump down

WEDDING BELLS AGAIN: Here I am in 1976 with my second wife Veronica. Everyone worried about the one legged man falling down, but I cruised through the ceremony and steps with out a hitch or noise from my suction socket leg . Looks like my wife just received a barrage of rice, but the ole infantryman did not even bat an eye!

with alcohol and gave it a good dusting of powder. I pulled on the slip sock and carefully pulled it out through the vacuum hole as my stump slid into the leg's willow wood socket. I pushed down and my stump slid into place with a slight hiss.

I walked around my room a bit and it was working fine. I finished dressing just as Oscar arrived. We went over to the church and I introduced Oscar to Father Byrolli. He took Oscar up to the balcony and introduced him to the organist. Oscar discussed his songs with the organist and then Father Byrolli showed Oscar his way down to the altar.

We more or less synchronized watches. Oscar went off to get ready and I went back to my house to wait. I was nervous, not about getting married, but about tripping over the edge of a carpet or something and making a fool of myself. Actually I didn't mind the later so much as I had done the fool part before, but I wanted everything to be nice and beautiful for my wife-to-be and my mother. My father had died of cancer about six years earlier.

Oscar returned wearing a new western style suit that Bonnie had bought for him. He was proud of it and it did look good on him. Well, it looked great all the way down to his ankles. There his pants were about two inches too long. This made his pants look a bit baggy. Oscar said he did not know what went wrong. They fit fine when he was measured up.

I looked down at his toes sticking out from under his cuffs and did not see the pointed toes of cowboy boots. Oscar most all of the time wore special boots. He even had a pair that had belonged to

Porter Wagner. I asked him what he had on his feet. I was right; he was wearing a shiny new pair of oxfords he had bought for the wedding.

Yes, that was why his pants were too long. He had been fitted with his boots on. Oscar said his boots were still in the trunk of his car. We both looked at our watches and agreed there was no time to spare to get them. He would have to go as is! It was time to "get me to the church on time!"

At the church everybody was there and waiting. Oscar went up to the organ in the balcony. I got into position just behind the curtain on the altar. Father Byrolli gave the signal and the ceremony began. The organ played and Oscar sang. He never sounded better.

The music paused and we waited for Oscar. He did not come. Father signaled the organist to play some more. Finally Oscar arrived. He came through the side door at full speed. He shot past the Father and shot past me. I reached out and grabbed him before he flew through the curtain!

Father Byrolli calmed us all down with a short prayer. The wedding march began. The curtain was parted and the three of us headed out on stage. Father turned left to the rostrum and Oscar and I proceeded down the narrow steps to the front of the altar. I made it with all of the grace that an above the knee amputee could expect.

I took a quick look at Oscar and noticed that he was disheveled. He explained that on running outside of the church he had slipped on some ice on the sidewalk and had fallen down! I looked from him to the center aisle and there was my beautiful bride-to-be being escorted by a very proud Uncle Joseph. I think it was the most beautiful sight I had ever seen.

My wife-to-be joined me and we turned to face the priest to receive our vows. Father Byrolli towered high above us. The Father was a tall lean man and from our angle looked even taller than he was. He made the first part of the ceremony from the pulpit then turned to come down for the ring ceremony and finishing touches.

As he approached the steps he tripped over something. It looked like he was coming right down on top of us. I wondered how I could catch such a large person and was steeling myself for the impact when somehow the good Father righted himself and continued on down to our level and completed the ceremony.

After the ceremony at the reception as we toasted the occasion with a glass of champagne, I reminded them that Oscar had fallen on the ice and Father Byrolli had almost gone head first off the altar. I, the one everyone was so worried about, had had no problems at all!

I was trying to explain that it wasn't a fart and rapping on my wooden leg to try and prove it, but he was so mad he did not hear a word. However, before he could take a good swing at me, Big Mac, the bartender, and a good friend stepped in. The man listened to Big Mac, who towered above him and it all ended with a big laugh from all involved. I was glad I was at my local watering hole. I decided I had to be more careful when coming down off a barstool.

# Chapter Sixteen

## Some Problems of a One-Legged Football Photog

I had been taking photographs as a hobby ever since the early days of high school and had my own darkroom with pretty good equipment. While going to the University of Maryland it was a natural for me to start taking photos for the Diamond Back, the school's bi-weekly newspaper. I had covered a variety of stories, but not much on sports except a few of individual players who had made All-American. One in soccer and the other in lacrosse. Then one day the sports editor asked me to cover a football game. I thought of all the walking and standing and started to back out, but ended up saying (to myself) "What the hell. Give it a try."

Football was my favorite sport and I had played it in high school. It seemed like years ago but was only about four. It was what had happened in between then and now that made it seem so far away. On my first trip to the dressing room I was surprised to be greeted by three players who remembered, and played with or against me in high school. Big Jim O'Brien and Wilbur Rock had also known me from Eddy's Friendly Tavern and during the war were part of a group called Eddy's Rangers. Wilbur had planted a flag saying the name of the place and its location in Washington, D.C. on the beach at Iwo Jima during the first wave of the invasion.

Well, that was a good start and an introduction to the whole team as well as the coaches. I know I was not as good of a player as they said I was, but who was I to argue the point. It was during the first game I photographed that I figured out a system to make sure I had a photo of the action.

There is a lot of walking back and forth on the side to follow the action on the field. A lot even for a two-legged person. I could walk along with the best of them, but I did get tired at times. Early on in the game I shot the action at the line of scrimmage where it was relatively easy to get a good action shot. I also was on a limited budget. The photographer from the papers and wire services were not. The Diamond Back would only pay for two or three negatives and one eight by ten enlargement unless something special happened.

By getting shots to cover the game early, I could then drop back and wait to shoot that big touchdown pass – the "game-winning" one. During one game I did this. Maryland had the ball. I shot a couple on the line of scrimmage and then feeling a little tired in my stump area, I walked about thirty yards down to the goal line where I could lean back against the stands and get a little rest while keeping my eye on what was going on. I had done this before, but no one had noticed. However, this time just seconds after I got along side the goal line Maryland's quarterback threw a pass. I was right there and got a great shot of what turned out to be the winning touchdown.

The whole group of sideline photographers came rushing down to the goal, but all they were able to get was the point-after kick. While the team was getting ready for the kick off a photographer from The Washington Star and The Daily News came over to ask me, "How come you got down here for that play?" I told them the truth, that my leg was tired so I just wandered down here to take it easy for a while. It was the truth, but they didn't believe it.

They first thought I had some sixth sense about the game, and then Krebbs said, "I got it! He can read the signals." The Star guy added, "or the coach tipped him off!" The more I tried to tell them what really happened the more they thought I was covering up. The word got around to all the photographers, "That Addor was reading the quarterbacks signals." The result was that every place I went up or down the field they followed like a swarm of ducklings after their mother.

I think, that day, they would have even followed me into the stadium restroom. This continued for several games and then finally, since I had made no more great scoops, they believed that I only got that photo because my stump was a little sore on the end. This system of covering myself with shots at scrimmage landed me a big time photo. It was during the second Gator Bowl, Maryland was playing West Virginia. The mountaineers were beat by more than just one touch down. This was about the second year that Jim Tatum had taken over as coach and Maryland was heading for the top spot in college football.

not crying out in pain. If you didn't know, it looked nasty. If you knew it looked funny.

I told the Maryland trainer that I was all right. My only problem was a leg bent a little at the knee. I said maybe one of you big guys could bend it back so it will work. Elmer got a hold of it down by the ankle and Stan held my leg just above the knee joint. I gave instructions while everybody including a team of stretcher-bearers stood around me in a circle.

I could hear the announcer off in the distance describing to the fans what was happening although he did not know any of the details or that I had an artificial leg. With a little effort the knee was back working. I go up and walked over and sat on a bench. The ref blew his whistle and the game went back in motion. It had been stopped for about fifteen minutes.

It had been quite an experience. The closest I had been to a football game since my last game back at Coolidge High in 1941. There was no television back then, only radio so I never got to see me in action. No one in the broadcast booth mentioned my name (I was an unknown photographer), but Mom and Dad sitting at home in Washington, D.C. heard it. They knew it was me.

I guess I did pretty well as a photographer at Maryland. I got to know most of the photographers from the Washington papers and some from the wire services. I met a tall blond guy who was covering this bowl game for Life magazine. I later worked with him on my first job as Public Information Officer at Walter Reed Army Medical Center. Here, if an army photographer was not available, I was asked to help out with my camera. I had been working at Walter Reed almost a year when I go a call from the photo editor of the Washington Post. He wanted me to come and work for them and take the place of a very good cameraman who had left to join AP photo service.

I said, "Who? Me!" He said, "Yes, we know your work." I said, "But. . ." He said we know about your leg too. I was highly flattered. Photography had always been a hobby that some times I used to make a few extra bucks. I thought about it and it was tempting. The pay was a lot more than I was getting working for the U.S. government and there were lots of side goodies like getting to belong to the White House Press Photographers Association. I said no and the Post Editor said, "Think it over please."

I did, but told him no again. I said I was honored to considered for a job as a photographer on such a great newspaper, but I went to college to learn to be a writer, a journalist and that was what I was going to do. He understood and wished me luck. I often wonder what it would have been like. Lots of glamour, but also a lot of stinky darkroom work. I am glad I kept my camera work as a hobby with a few free-lance jobs here and there throughout the years.

# Chapter Seventeen

## Or How Rehabilitated Can One Get?

A couple of years after Dad died Mother and I were invited to Uncle Bill's 50th wedding anniversary. Uncle Bill was Mother's youngest brother and had been a very close uncle to me. So, it was not only a family must, but also a great pleasure. I picked up Mother at Warwic Towers where she had been staying since Dad's death and we headed up Georgia Avenue towards Leisure World where the 50th wedding anniversary of Uncle bill and Aunt Silvia was to be held.

The traffic was bad. It is always bad on Saturday afternoon. Almost worse than rush hour during the week. We finally got to Leisure World and found the parking lot jammed. Not only does the place have several halls they rent, but also the weekends bring visitors to the many residents. Around and around the parking lot I went, but no luck. Then, as I was starting to make my umpteenth tour of the lot I saw a car pull out of a parking place almost in front of the entrance.

I revved up the engine and made a dash for it. As I started to pull into the place, my mother suddenly said, "You can't park there. It's marked for handicapped!" I started to stop and back out but remembered who I was and replied, "Mom, I am handicapped." We both had a good laugh. I parked the car and we went in and had a great afternoon helping Uncle Bill and Aunt Silvia celebrate 50 years of marriage.

At this time in my life I seldom used the handicapped parking places. I had a handicapped tag from Delaware. Actually it was a DAV tag (Disabled American Veteran) and amounted to the same thing as far as parking places were concerned. I left such places for those that had more problems in walking than I did. I could walk from most anywhere on any parking lot to the place I was going.

The Pentagon might be an exception to this. It has acres and acres of parking lot and some a very long distance from the building. Later I used the special parking places for two reasons. First, there was a great influx of handicapped parking license plates for almost anyone who had reached the senior citizen age and who complained about having a hard time walking to their doctor.

The other was that time was catching up with me and it was easier not to walk any greater distance than I had to. Maybe I was getting lazy. I don't really know, but when Spring came around I would curb this urge and park at the other end of the parking lot to build up my strength and walking ability for the good times coming with the summer weather. Like walking the boardwalk at Rehoboth Beach with my young son and family.

# Chapter Eighteen

## Me, A Man of Iron

Here are a few times when having an artificial leg worked to my advantage. When getting out of a car or just opening the door, the door will have a tendency to want to come back on you and close itself. In my two-legged days I caught this rebound with a hand so that it would not wang my shinbone and cause a cut or bruise.

I discovered a new way to check a car door after I had been wearing my artificial leg for only a short time. I would fling the door open and when it bounced back I would catch it on my "wooden" shin. (For many years, before plastics moved in, my leg was made from lightweight willow wood). This became a natural reflex.

A couple of times people close by would wince when the door hit my shin. Finally one day a fellow who had gone through the wincing routine came over and asked why I had not even flinched. He said, "You must be a very tough guy!" I laughed and rapped on my leg to show him that it was artificial. He laughed also and headed off to do

I thought maybe he wanted me to pay for the damage so I was reaching for my checkbook when he said the beer was on the house. You don't owe me anything. Then he asked the question that had been bugging him and customers for two years. "How the hell could you have put you knee through that glass brick and walk out of here with out a murmur or slightest limp?" He added, "Man, what are you made of!"

I stepped back from the bar a bit and pulled up my right pant leg to show him my artificial leg. I pointed to the heavy metal "hinge" on each side of the knee and said those are what broke the glass brick. He laughed. We all laughed. I offered to pay for the damage saying I had no money or checkbook with me when it happened. He said not to worry, insurance paid for it and besides the story was worth the cost of fixing it anyhow.

Joe and I had another cold one and left the Bucket of Blood and never returned.

Another time when my knee wanged something it was more personal. I was still in the army at Walter Reed and in uniform; I was taking leave from the hospital to visit a friend in New York City. Our country's rail system had taken a beating during the war years as repair work and materials all went to the fighting zones. Thus, the train car I was in had gotten a little rickety and worn as Washington to NYC was, and is, a much used railroad line.

I got up from my seat to go to the men's room. About halfway down the aisle I saw a full bird colonel coming towards me. I was a PFC, private first class. I debated a salute, but realized the situation did not call for one. As the officer came alongside I tried to make myself "skinny" but as we were side-by-side the train hit a bump or something and I lurched right into him.

As I said, "Excuse me, Sir," I felt my artificial knee hit him in his knee area. I also heard him let out a yelp. I said another "Sorry Sir!" and kept on going to the restroom. I had a job that had to be done. Shortly after I returned to my seat the colonel came up the aisle to me still limping. He asked a question that went something like this, "What the hell are you made of soldier?"

I showed him my artificial knee and he said, "Oh, That's a great weapon!" I told him that I had lost my leg from wounds received at Bastogne, Belgium during the Battle of the Bulge. He offered his regrets and wanted to buy me a drink, but I declined with "Thanks, but no thanks." I didn't want to push my luck and besides it was too early in the day for a beer.

# Chapter Nineteen

## -Have a Little Understanding of Others

I discovered early on that you can describe war to people, or they can even see documentary movies, but the only ones who really understand what war is like are those who have been there and experienced its hell. It is also that way about being an amputee. You have to be one to understand how it feels to face a two-legged world.

Even then it is different with each individual. We all see things from our point of view. A point of view made up from our background from childhood to present. Also the experiences we have faced during our lifetime leave their mark, good or bad, on each of us. So have a little understanding for a friend or family member who can't quite adjust to the fact that his friend or loved one is now different from when he knew him with his full set of limbs.

One day many years ago shortly after I had received my artificial leg and discharge from the army I had to remind my mother of this fact.

My mother enjoyed playing bridge and belonged to several local bridge clubs. One day when mother was host for a club made up of local "Girls" one of the players asked her how I was doing. My Mother said something like, "Very well. Thank you, but it's quite a task getting around that large campus at the University of Maryland."

Before the lady who had asked the question could reply, a good neighbor up the street said, "Well! He's got an artificial leg doesn't he?" Her tone was like why worry the new leg will take care of everything! This made my mother very angry. She and Amy had been friends and neighbors for many years. However, mother being very much a lady and the party's host let it pass.

When I got home from school I saw at once that something was bothering her. I asked what had happened. She told me what Amy C. had said and about her brusque tone. She said that she never wanted to see Amy again!

I said, "Mom, don't be so hard on Amy. She is a very nice lady and did not mean any harm. She just doesn't know or understand the problems that an amputee may or may not have. Many well meaning people do not! It's like the war. You have to really be there to understand what it feels like.

Of course being close to either one helps a lot with understanding. You are close to me. You are my mother. Thus you have a greater understanding about the problems I and the guys on ward-10A have than anyone else except maybe Dad. I also reminded her that her friends voice often sounded gruff for no reason at all.

I'm glad to say that Mom thought it over and came to agree with me, She forgave her good friend and their friendship continued for many more years.

Here is another time that I ran across someone who did not really understand an amputees problem with an above the knee prosthesis.

During World War II there was a great housing shortage in our Nation's Capital. Homeowners, who had an extra room, were asked to rent it to help ease this shortage. This policy continued for a couple of years after the war.

The Veterans Administration set up a special orthopedic board or committee to work on and study improvements in artificial limbs. Experts in the field volunteered to serve their country and those wounded in the war. They were called "One Dollar a Year Men." One such expert was rooming with neighbors across the street from where I lived.

We got to know each other and often had a chat as to how I used my leg and various problems I had walking on my wooden leg. It turned out that he was with a group of scientists who were trying to improve the artificial knee joint. They already knew that one of our biggest problems was going up and down stairs. The only way was to step up with the real leg and then bring the artificial leg up to it. It made climbing stairs much slower than it would have been with two good healthy legs.

One day when I was getting out of my car on returning home from Maryland the very excited Dollar-a Year-Man came running over to see me. He told me that they had begun working on a wonderful new idea for an artificial knee based on hydraulics. I said great!

As we moved into my house he added you would be able to go up stairs the regular way, foot over foot! He went on telling me about

them all together with their truck when not fighting a fire. During one of the fires I heard the man on the radio making some statements that were not exactly right legally. I mentioned it to the Chief telling him what was wrong.

I am a retired journalist and had for four years been the public information officer for Walter Reed Army Medical Center in Washington, D.C. There are certain laws of privacy concerning an accident or hospital patient that should be followed to avoid any possibility of a lawsuit. I also told him that I was a qualified communications technician in the Coast Guard Auxiliary. Now I was no Marconi, but I did know how to operate most radios as well as the proper manner of speaking into them.

The Chief liked that and I became the head radio guy for the fire company. To me this was a lot more interesting then taking portraits of burning bushes or barns. I also became a dispatcher seeing that the correct engines went out on call and the ones not needed stayed put in case another alarm sounded.

I was the member living closest to the firehouse so unless somebody was in the place when the alarm went off, I was usually the first to arrive. I would unlock and enter the rear door and head for the office. The first thing I did was to check in with emergency headquarters to inform them that we were in the process of answering the call and find out more details about the fire or accident.

I then went and opened the front overhead doors just about the time the firemen were arriving. Usually by then our chief had phoned in to ask for details and to give me instructions regarding which engines to take. He worked as a repairman for Sears appliances and with permission from the company had one of our "home radios" in his truck. He usually met the firemen at the scene.

Being a rural fire station there were not many fire plugs at the location of our fires.

Instead stations in our area depended on the station's tank truck to refill the pumpers when they went "dry". When a tanker got empty it had to come back to the station for a refill. This meant I often had to contact a nearby station requesting tanker service while our truck was being filled. It takes a lot longer to refill one of these large water carriers than it does to empty it.

While waiting for the tanker to return I stretched out the long filling hose and attached it to our well pump. To do this I had to walk backward while pulling on the fire-hose. At the time I was wearing a suction socket above the knee leg. I had to be very careful as I stepped back that my mechanical knee joint was all the way back or the leg would fold on me and down I would go. I don't remember this ever happening, but I had some close calls.

Later I got a new type of peg leg that the Veterans Administration called a "sports leg." An amputee veteran of the Vietnam War had requested it. I got mine because I found it easier to do heavy yard work not having to worry about a knee bending or a honeysuckle vine tripping me up. It also made working around the firehouse and laying our hose a lot easier and faster. I still wear this peg leg, but now as my only leg. Old age made it too hard on my hands to pull the slip sock through the bottom of my suction socket leg.

My wife also asked me to wear the "peg" when we went up to the clubhouse as I could dance better on it. Actually, I have found that I can do most everything using my peg leg that I could do with the real looking artificial one. Some of the exceptions were things that one did in a sitting position. Sitting on a bar stool at the bar was one. Also when in a car and at a dinner table when others were around. Without the knee joint the leg sticks straight out in front of me. However, it does come apart at the knee area so that the above can be accomplished. It just takes a little time to remove a large plastic bolt that joins the two parts.

I never got to be a full-fledged certified fire fighter. For that you had to attend three days of the Delaware State Fire School. I had practiced going up and down a ladder and could do it fairly well. Actually there were not many fires that required ladder work in our area, but the fire school required it. I talked it over with my fire chief and one of the instructors at the school. They both encouraged me to do it, so I registered for the next class. Unfortunately, my wife got seriously ill and all thoughts of the fire school were dropped to take care of her.

I was still an active fireman, certified or not, and answered every call that I could. I also attended the meetings and helped in decisions concerning the business of running a fire station. I did this until my wife died. I then moved out of our fire company's district. On my last meeting night I turned in my running gear and radio. I handed the chief my badge and identification as a member of the Indian River Volunteer Fire Company. He handed it back to me and said to hold it for a while.

During the meeting I was amazed and deeply touched when they presented me a plaque making me a "Life Member" of the company. I cannot put into words the pride and other emotions I felt at this honor. The feeling was very much the same as when after five years at the University of Maryland I walked across the stage and received my diploma.

I found out that in the beginning while I was wearing my regular leg with a shoe on the end, nobody realized that I was wearing an artificial leg. This awakening occurred one hot summer day. I was cutting grass and wearing shorts when the alarm sounded. Since it was Saturday several of the men, including Chief Mosley, were working at the firehouse. Thus for a change I was not the first there.

When I walked through the big front door Chief Mosley was heading for our number one pumper. When he saw me, or rather my artificial leg swinging in the breeze, he stopped dead in his tracks. He kind of stammered and with the sound of apology in his voice, said to me, "I didn't know you had one of those...I mean an artificial leg." He added that he was sorry. I said for what? He said later that he noticed I had a slight limp, but thought no more of it.

I thanked him and told him he had just given me, and any amputee, especially an above the knee one, the highest compliment a person could give. That is, not being able to tell that I was using an artificial leg. I had not planned on being a fireman. Nor did I go into it as a challenge. I just joined in with friends and did the best I could.

I was never sure if I had pulled my own weight with the company until I was presented that life membership. That's one reason it meant so much to me.

# Chapter Twenty-One

## I Join the Coast Guard Auxiliary

I don't know exactly why, but I had never thought much about boating. I did own and use a 17-foot outboard motorboat for a few years when my twelve-year old son got the fishing bug. I, along with my son, took the Coast Guard Auxiliary Safe Boating course as the boat dealer had recommended it.

However, when I got married for the second time in 1976, I was retired and we were living in the Rehoboth Beach area, my wife decided she would like to have a boat and join the Indian River Yacht club, or it could have been the other way around. I can't remember the sequence of these events.

I had always enjoyed all aspects of the water, so I agreed. I was thinking along the lines of a nice outboard similar to the one my son and I had called "Blow Fish." My wife had other ideas. She located an almost 30-foot cabin cruiser that she "just had to have". Since we were not the first owners it came at a price that would not bust my budget.

We got a slip at the yacht club, but it was at least 250 feet out in the Indian River near the end of the pier. Closer in the water was too shallow. There was not much deep water in Warwick Cove. In fact at times when the tide was running real low one had to wait for it to turn and come back in for safe cruising to the river's channel.

I soon found that boating on a small yacht was another challenge to my prosthesis and me. The catwalks that ran down the side of the slips were a little too narrow for my liking, but a railing built by a carpenter friend of mine put that worry to rest. The next problem was getting on and off of our wonderful little boat.

My wife had named her "Macushla", Gaelic for sweetheart. My Veronica was half Irish and could speak the tongue. There was only a short time when the gunwale of the boat was even with the dock or close to it. At all other times it was difficult for me to get aboard my boat, but somehow I managed. Onboard the distance from gunwale to deck was around three feet, but this did not vary with the tide. I made a sturdy, but small portable set of wooden steps to help me descend and ascend into and out of Macushla.

It didn't take me very long to find ways to get around my boat. The peg leg worked a lot better than the suction socket with its mechanical knee, so I became known as "Ole Peg Leg the Pirate." They, my friends and fellow sailors, from the club thought it would be great if I wore an eye patch. However, I didn't go along with that.

One day a young friend of mine stopped me as I was heading down the dock and for home and asked me if I would like to join the Coast Guard Auxiliary. I said that it sounded interesting, but I did not know anything about it. He steered me into the bar and bought me a beer. As we drank a frosty mug Keith told me all about the organization.

When he was through with his recruiting pitch I was sold. I told him that I had been in the army for three years, worked for them as a civilian for four and had been an editor on a navy magazine for more than seventeen years so why not the Coast Guard, or at least the Auxiliary. My wife thought it was a great idea so I was soon voted in as a member of the Indian River Flotilla

I helped with inspection of boats for water safety and also participated by teaching a bit at the CGAUX Safe Boating classes. Here, my years as editor and writer on a US Navy magazine put me in good steed. The most enjoyable of the Flotilla's duties was patrolling the area waters to help boats in distress.

When I first joined we were able to patrol the Atlantic Ocean from the Indian River Inlet north to the Delaware Bay. In these waters Macushla could cruise with ease and be ready to lend a hand to anyone in distress. However, for some reason unknown to me the Coast Guard took the ocean patrolling away from us and did it themselves.

Some said it was too dangerous for "civilians" to patrol. That doesn't add up as our training was as good as theirs and in some cases seemed even better. That just about put my boat and I out of the patrolling business. Except for the channel the water was too shallow for me to reach a boat in need of help. Likewise Rehoboth Bay.

The Coast Guard Auxiliary is a fine organization of civilians with boating skills and boats. During my ten years as a member I never did feel that the Coast Guard or government made full use of the abilities of this organization particularly in time of emergency or when a tight water security was needed. I hope this has changed as both the CGAUX and the Power Squadron could and should be a big help in fighting terrorists.

I had to learn some new techniques in walking on my artificial leg to be a good sailor. Walking or moving about on a small boat can be difficult even for those with two good legs. Some things at first seemed impossible for me to do, but I figured out a way to do them. This was not always the tried and true or official way, but "Ole Peg Leg" got the job done.

# Chapter Twenty-Two

## I Become a Race Car Driver

It was back in 1956 or '57 and I was sitting one Saturday afternoon in my home on Insley Street in Silver Spring, Maryland. My wife was doing something in the kitchen that would probably become dinner later in the day. I was reading the sports section of the Evening Star when an ad caught my attention. The ad featured photos of some sleek new little sports cars. I had seen an MG on my way to work and a jaguar tooling down 16th Street the other day. The cars in the ads were Triumphs, a car I had never heard of.

This was just the beginning of the time that would later be called a sports car craze, as these speedy little cars from England began to be seen on our streets. I looked at the name of the dealership and it said United Autos, Wheaton Maryland. I realized that the address must be that of the old Chevy dealership that had moved to new quarters out on Georgia Avenue. While I was pondering this, my wife hollered from the kitchen that she was out of cigarettes. Would I go and get her some? I said, "Wow!" Not out loud, just to myself and said, "Why sure dear."

I got in the passengers seat next to Dick and Sharon, skates and all, fit nicely in the space behind on a small jump seat. We left the dealership and headed to the Wheaton Pharmacy for the cigarettes. This done we headed back down Georgia Avenue to Caroll Knolls. The top was down. The sun was warm and the sky was blue with beautiful puffy clouds. Dick showed me how he put it through the gears. All four of them, but explained that fourth gear was only used at high speeds on the open road. You had to keep your RPM's up or you would "lug" the engine and you could bend a pushrod. Also you would waste a lot of power and gasoline. All of this was great, but the feeling of traveling so low to the street in a car that fit you almost like underwear was what truly gave me a thrill. It was a totally new experience for me and I loved it.

We pulled up in front of my house on Insley Street and Dick honked the horn. I met my wife half way to the curb and handed her the cigarettes. She hardly noticed them and headed right for the bright red car. By that time there was quite a gathering of neighbors also admiring the car and asking questions about it. Sharon had jumped out and was telling her Mom how wonderful the ride had been. Dick asked my wife to jump in. She did and off they went for a cruise. When they came back Dick gave every one else who asked to go, a ride. Dick had been right. My wife had completely forgotten how long I had been gone. She was having a ball being the center of attention and experiencing something new.

All of this was great, but I had a feeling that the pretty little car would be too expensive to fit our budget. Also, just two seats was impractical for a one car family man, but the biggest thing was that with my right leg gone above the knee I would never be able to drive it. Before we left to go back to pick up my car Dick asked me if I still "took pictures." I said, "Yes! I still have my Speedgraphic and a darkroom in my basement." Dick then asked me if I would like to photograph his racing team in action. "I sure would!" I replied, "but will have to ask my wife."

Now, this sounds like I'm "hen-pecked," but I don't think so. I just like approval from my wife for anything that will take me away from my family. She agreed, so plans were made for me to join the United Autos Triumph Racing Team at the next local race at Upper Marlboro, Maryland. This was about a month away so I had plenty of time to prepare.

I had been a fan of local stock car racing and had attended many races at local ovals. This had always been from the stands and I had never been down close to the action. Road racing was different and sure seemed more interesting. I spent a lot of time at the dealership learning about sports cars and meeting new friends from Dick's staff.

When the time came for my first sports car race, and I was out trackside at Marlboro's two mile simulated road course, I was sold on the sport. In fact I was hooked on anything sports car. However, it did make me feel the loss of my leg again, but I did not let that stop me from enjoying the race. At least with my camera I could be part of a racing team. Not exactly the same thing, but fun nonetheless. It was kind of like when I was back at the University of Maryland taking photos of the football team and the game. I had loved football also, but now had to enjoy it vicariously. My camera brought me closer to the game as well as the racing.

I had purchased a Renault 4-CV from United Autos and was using it as my every day car. It had what the French called a Ferlic Clutch. It was more or less an electric clutch that when you pushed down on the gearshift lever you could change gears. This got me back to the fun of shifting gears again and it was a neat looking small foreign car, but not a racer, although it had a lot of pep.

It was a great car to drive through Washington's rush hour traffic and it got at least 38 miles per gallon even while carrying three passengers. When a race was away from our local track I followed the Triumphs of United Autos there. As I have said before, the little car was very fast for its make. Some thought it had been modified by one of Dick's racing mechanics but it was pure stock, just the way it came from the factory.

I did ok keeping up with our "caravan", until the guys in the TRs exceeded 70 mph. At that speed my 4-CV was all but flying and would not hold the road very well. When I caught up to them at our destiny, they would tease me saying things like, "Why don't you get a real car?" I came right back at them with "If I could drive one of them "blankety, blank," vehicles you know "blank" well I would." Of course this was all in good fun and they would buy me a beer to prove it. So it went for several years, me, my little Renault and camera following The United Autos Racing Team from track to track. I became active in the Washington, D.C. region of the Sports Car Club of America in most every way but driving. I even put out the club's newsletter a few times when the regular editor was not available. ·

At some point during this period I had divorced my wife. However, the reasons had nothing to do with my sports car activities! I had moved to an efficiency apartment over a two-car garage not far from where I had lived so I could be close to my son. Not only was the apartment a short drive from my son and former home, but, it was also on several acres of woods with a creek right next to my driveway and a couple of frisky raccoons as neighbors.

While driving my Renault to work and around town many people asked me about it and I gave several demonstrations. I made a deal with United Autos as a part time salesman. When I talked to a person about my car I would give them one of the dealer's business cards with my name stamped on the back of it. If they then bought a car, I received a commission.

One day after work I pulled into the dealers parking lot and went inside to see if I had sold any cars this week. As I entered the showroom the owner, Dick Pelicano, the head salesman, Walt Hutchenson and most of the staff, immediately surrounded me. They all had grins on their faces that would have out done the Cheshire Cat's grin to shame. I asked, "What's going on?" Hutch shoved a clipboard in front of me and asked me that same old question, "Why don't you buy a really good car?"

TR-3A with all of the things on it that were hard to get figuring that the longer it took to get the car the more money I could round up particularly if the time included another pay check. I used my car for a down payment, not because I had to, but to make the purchase easier. I went back to my apartment that evening feeling great, but a little worried about the money I had just contracted to spend. Then I thought of the time I had to gather in funds and how great it would be to be behind the wheel of a sports car. I hoped that funny clutch would work as well as Jack said it would.

Well, my car came in three days. Dick had put a special on it. I went up to look at it and there it was in beautiful bright red with black leather interior. Jack was busy working on it to install his "vacuum clutch" and getting it ready to purr. He said it would be ready the next day. I settled up with Hutch signing a whole mess of papers and walked out on cloud nine.

The next day the car was ready as promised and Jack took me for a ride to explain not only how the clutch worked, but also the proper way to drive a sports car. The main point was to watch your RPMs (revolutions per minute) on the tachometer and to not hurry through the gears like most people do with a big old Detroit car. Jack pointed out that I shouldn't use fourth gear unless I was out on the road doing 50 or more. The point of keeping the RPMs up in each gear was not to "lug" the engine and possibly bend a push rod or waste a lot of gas.

I caught on quick. The clutch button on top of the gearshift lever worked great. It was the trigger mechanism from a WW II fighter plane. On the plane you pushed the button in and bullets flew out.

On my car you pushed the button in and the clutch went in. Then shift gears, let off the button and out came the clutch.

There was an adjustment under the hood so that the speed of the clutch coming out could be regulated according to use. Slower while driving to and from work in rush hour traffic and faster for more open driving and racing. However at this time I had no thoughts of entering competition. Just driving this great handling car and enjoying shifting gears again, a thing that I thought was gone for good, was enough.

The notice came out about the spring race driving school that our club was going to hold. In order to race in the Sports Club of America events you had to have an SCCA (Sports Car Club of America) driving or rather racing license. To get this, one had to go to an approved driving school that usually was given on a long weekend. First you got a novice license and then after competing in a specified number of novice races a regular or national license would be issued and you could run with the big boys. The Washington Region was authorized to hold such schools, in fact the schools they held were considered to be among the best in the country.

I don't know exactly why or how I decided I wanted to go to racing school, but I did. I didn't tell my family. Mom didn't understand racing. To her cars were for getting from here to there. She would also wonder why someone who was almost killed on the battlefield and had an artificial leg would want to risk his life speeding around a track with a bunch of other nuts. I often wondered the same thing also.

Now both the car and I had to be made ready. I had filled out the application and needed a medical exam to ok my health, to certify I was all right to drive in races. This mostly meant is my heart steady and was I prone to seizures? This was a bit of a problem, as I had no "family doctor". All of my medical care since I had lost my leg came through the Veterans Hospital and this wasn't exactly a thing they covered. At this time most doctors in the Washington, D.C area only took strangers from a recommended patient of their own and then only under due cause. I called a few from the phone book with no results. Then I went up to a doctor's office near where I had lived, asked and got my physical.

Now that I had a doc's statement that I was healthy enough to participate in racing I ran into another problem, The Regional Officers. Did National SCCA rules have a regulation concerning one-legged drivers? Seems that I was kind of a first. They also wondered if my special controls would be accepted in the Production Class for Triumphs or would I have to run in modified and be out classed by really "hot" cars.

The racing committee composed of club members with SCCA racing experience, convened to discuss the matter with me and make a decision. Now these were friends of mine and they were not trying to prevent me from racing, but rather trying to determine how I could get out on the track in accordance with SCCA's racing and safety rules.

After searching through many books of rules and regulations they came to the conclusion that there was nothing there to prevent me from racing. In fact there was nothing there at all about one-legged or handicapped drivers. One of the members of the committee, Dick Thompson, had been a friend of my family for years. Mom went to high school with both Dick's mother and father and they often played bridge together. Now Dick was a few years older than I was so we had never met until recently, but felt like we had known each other closer through our parents talk.

Dick finally broke the deadlock by saying, "His car is built for him to drive and there are no rules that say no! So let's put him on the track and see how both he and the car work out." All agreed and I was set for race driving school. They wished me luck and I left feeling elated, but a bit nervous too.

Next I had to get the proper gear for my TR and me. In those early days of sports car racing in the U.S. there were not many suppliers of racing stuff. At least not around the Washington, D.C area. Jack found a roll bar out of a Triumph that had been wrecked and installed it. Racing shocks were not required, but highly recommended. I had ordered those on my car when I bought it, as I like the stiffer ride. The helmet became a problem. A national safety rule had been made by SCCA that required all helmets to have been approved by the Snell Foundation for safety in a crash.

Current drivers had until this July to comply, but all new drivers had to have a helmet with a Snell approved seal in it. A big source for helmets had been the Air Force or motorcycle police suppliers. But these all flunked the Snell safety tests. To make matters worse I have a large, 7 ½, head size. Finally, Dick Thompson came up with a helmet that was approved and would fit. I had a feeling that it might have been a spare one of his, but it was brand new.

Friday, the first day of the school, was all in the classroom where we learned the rules and regulations and what the different colored flags meant. Or course every one knew what the checkered clothe meant. Also that the green meant go, but there were others like yellow, red, yellow with a blue stripe and a red with a black ball in the center and there was also a plain black flag. We were also taught the theory of cornering and were shown how to negotiate the corners on the two-mile course outside on a big layout of the track. That all seemed easy enough to me as most was just common sense. I knew the doing of it would be different and hoped I would be able to handle my car with its special controls ok. I also hoped that the controls would hold up under the extremes of racing.

Saturday morning turned out to be a very nice day with lots of sunshine and white puffy clouds floating through a blue, blue sky. Along with the other class members, I reported to the track's starting line in front of the empty grandstand. The group walked around the two-mile twisty course to get a close up look at the track's surface, banks and turns.

Two miles was a bit too far for me to walk so they let me follow behind in my car. This gave me a general idea of what the track was like, but I could not hear the words of the instructor. However, during Friday's classroom instructions we had studied the theories of cornering and had "applied" them to a diagram of the racecourse so now I knew what the track was like, at least at a slow pace. Speed would come later.

After this an experienced SCCA driver was assigned to each novice. He would drive the student around the track for a while explaining what he was doing and why. When he thought his student was ready he pulled into the pits and his student went out on his own to try his skills at the wheel. We were also told that speed alone around the course was not the only part of one's grade. More important was how one handled his car and how much he was aware of what was going on around him. This included other cars and signals from the flagmen at the corners.

It wasn't the time to try and blow every one else off the track.

Two MG's and an Austin Healy had pulled out onto the circuit while I sat in my TR-3 waiting. As I had expected, my instructor was Dick Thompson. He walked up to the car with his helmet in his hand, gave me a big "Hello" and smile and asked me if I thought he could drive my car. He was referring to the special controls. I said, "Hell, Dick if you can't I sure can't". He laughed and climbed into the drivers seat. I showed him the round knob with the button in the center mount on top of the gearshift lever. I told him, "push it in and the clutch goes in. Let your finger off the button the button comes out and so does the clutch. That's all there is to it." He started the engine and squeezed the button, pulled the lever down to low, let it out and we were off.

It was a funny feeling to me as I had seldom ridden in the passenger seat. I had always been the driver. Dick pulled up to the track entrance from the pits and waited for the flagman to wave the green. When he did Dick was off. Not like a "Bat out of Hell," as I thought he might, but slowly and smoothly. Around the oval and through the gears, at least the first three, then over the oval's bank on to the road course. The first time around was at about 40 miles per hour. The second was faster and after we rounded the hairpin turn and entered the quarter of a mile back stretch, Dick tapped me on my shoulder and pointed down at my special gear shifter, gave me an ok hand sign and floored the Triumph's gas pedal.

We streaked towards the left hand right angle turn at the end of the straightaway. Dick down shifted and around that corner we went. Up shift and more speed down the next part of the track. I could not hear my tires scream, but I could smell them smoking as Dick Thompson, one of our nation's top ten drivers, took my little red Triumph around that twisty two mile race course. I had wondered how I would react at top speeds in my car. Part of me hoped that I would chicken out and I would go back to being just a race photographer. The sensible thing for a 34-year old one-legged war vet to do.

I got goose bumps. Lots of goose bumps, but no chicken bumps. They were from the thrill of the high-speed chase, gear shifting and braking. Dick was having a ball with my vacuum controlled shifter and around and around we went faster and faster. I thought, "Wow! If I can ever get this buggy even close to this I'll be a winner."

Finally Dick geared down and we pulled into the pits. We had been out so long that we had run into lunchtime so I would have to wait until later to try my hand at the wheel. I also discovered that there had been quite an audience watching Dick Thompson in a Triumph TR-3 instead of one of his Corvettes.

I was on my crutches as I had decided that my artificial willow wood leg might get in the way at high speeds with twisty turns.

Also if I did spin out or hit someone, or they hit me, it might drive all of that wood up my ass. Well, not exactly, but I could do a lot of damage to my hip joint. During normal driving there was a small channel along the transmission hump to the motor and to the right of the gas pedal where I rested my prosthesis.

This put my artificial foot very close to the gas pedal and I felt that during the race my fake foot could slide over and get in the way. At 100 miles per hour this could spell disaster so I left it parked some place nearby when on the track. I put my crutches in the trunk of the TR and then hopped around to swing myself into the driver's seat. I was a pretty good hopper back then.

My friend and helper Ted Penn some times referred to me as "Hop-along Cassidy" a cowboy movie star of a few years back.

The simulated road course here at Upper Marlboro had been built off of a third of a mile high-banked oval of black asphalt. It used the back side of the oval and its north high bank and then the straight stretch in front of the grandstand where the start-finish line was placed and the chief flagman started the race with the wave of a green flag and ended it with a flourish of the checkered. At the end of the front stretch the course left the oval by exiting over the top of the high bank. This is where the road course addition began. It went down through an "S" turn and then a hairpin turn to the left and up the quarter mile back stretch.

At the end of that straight bit of running was a left ninety-degree bend and then a shorter stretch with a "dogleg" in it. Then two sharp lefts and a bit of a straight that ran into a right hand turn of about ninety degrees with a reverse camber. Then down behind the backside of the oval, behind, not on it, to a diminishing radius curve that led you up and back on to the oval and around the high bank to the finish line.

It was a tight gear-shifting lap with only the backstretch to get the car up to speed. Some of the experienced drivers loved it as a true test of driving skills while others driving bigger machines complained that it was too small with no place to unleash all of that expensive horsepower.

Some of the guys went on into Upper Marlboro for lunch at the Hotel or Marlboro Inn, but I opted for the refreshment stand in the pits, the center of the oval, and had a hamburger and a large coffee. This concession was run by the track owners as were the ones under the grandstands. During races it was the main source of nourishment for drivers and their pit crews. They sold hotdogs and hamburgers, coffee and in hot times ice tea. The burgers were not the best in the world, but were big and had a good and distinctive flavor. They were often referred to as "marlburgers." Through the next ten years I became rather fond of them and there was nothing as refreshing as a cold glass of ice tea during summer races when temperatures in the center of the oval often soared to 100 degrees or more.

Back at my car I sat and waited for the afternoon practice to begin. To say I was a bit nervous would be an understatement. I again wondered what I was doing here. Hadn't I done enough for a one-legged man already just by getting back to a normal life routine. I wasn't worried about crashing and getting hurt or dead.

I was worried about getting out there and making an ass of myself. All of my life I had worried about this and that people would laugh at me. I don't know why. They never have, at least to my knowledge. My thoughts were interrupted by the return of students and instructors. Dick came over to me and said action would start in about five minutes so get ready. He also told me to take it easy and gradually build up my speed as I got the feel of it. I agreed with him and he slapped me on the back and said, "Go get them."

My turn came. I got the green flag and around the oval I went shifting up to third. Off the oval I went and down through what was referred to as "the shoot." I went airborne and came down with a kerplunk, but smoothly. The "S" turn was on me almost at once. A sharp left and a sharp right. I got through it ok and started to down shift for the hairpin where top speed was only about 30 mph.

I tried to go through the turn in second and realized I should have gone all of the way down to low to have more power to dig out for the back stretch. This was almost like a quarter mile drag run except one had to make a ninety degree left at the end. Keep straight and you would crash through brush and wind up in the creek. I knew this. I had seen it happen. No one got hurt, but it was mighty sloppy and not recommended as good for the car.

The rest of my first lap around the track went a little smoother. I kept my eye on the tachometer and did a better job of keeping the "revs" up. I certainly didn't set any speed record but I didn't spin out or mess up in any other way. The second time around was a lot better. I was beginning to get the hang of it. The feel for it! After my first lap I realized it had been a smart move to leave the wooden leg

In my eagerness I almost ran over the car in front of me, but hit my brakes in time to avoid any contact. I had never seen so much confusion in traffic before. I'm not sure what I did or any of the other drivers did, but somehow I was through that mess and was shifting into high going up the backstretch. That first lap of my racing career I think was the most difficult one I ever faced.

During practice all we had to do was watch the track and keep an eye on the tachometer, or rather the red line. Now during the "real thing" one had to also watch the traffic. One also had to figure who had the right to the best groove in each turn. This was supposed to be the first one entering, but at speeds often over 100 mph that was not always so easy to determine. When in doubt I yielded.

This was my first race and I wanted to finish it. More aggressive driving could come later. After about five laps the tension running through my body began to ease up. Hey! I was still on the track. I had not run into anybody nor had anyone hit me. I relaxed and began to enjoy what I was doing.

I concentrated on each turn and tried to make each pass through it a little faster. I also set my eyes on the car in front of me and tried to catch and pass it. I also learned to watch my rearview mirror and waved faster cars to go on by. This was the driving school race so it had a variety of cars in it including a couple of Corvettes and a Ferrari.

I passed some cars and some cars passed me. I didn't win a trophy, but I sure had a great time and couldn't wait for the next race to come.

Well that's how I got into sports car racing. I ran in local and national races at Marlboro and the big Spring event on the airport at Cumberland, Maryland. Actually the airport is across the river in "West-By-God-Virginia," but it services Cumberland. I also attended the first two races held at the Virginia International Raceway (VIR) and Vineland, New Jersey. I also almost made a race in North Hampton, New Jersey, but they had rescheduled my race and due to heavy traffic on the Long Island Expressway we got there just in time to see the last lap.

I raced from 1959 to 1969. I had lots of fun and exercise. I never won a race, but was proud when I came in in fifth place a couple of times. About two years into racing, Bob Tulius, who was usually up front in his TR-4, asked me to join him and a friend, also a TR driver, to go racing full time. They were both going to quit their good job and devote themselves entirely to the sport they loved. Now this was in the 60's before the Sports Car Club of America allowed any money in races. We just raced for points and pretty silver trophies. It was quite a gamble. Bob said there were ways to get money from sponsors without breaking any SCCA rules.

I was surprised and flattered to be asked to join this new racing group. Bob had been a national champion in E production for several years. I looked at him in disbelief and said, "I've never even finished a race in the top five!" His immediate answer was, "Did you ever look at who was in front of you?" These drivers were: Mark Donahue in his Elva. Mark went on to drive for Roger Penske and win the Indianapolis 500 and many other races before being killed during practice for the Spanish Grand Prix in 1975. Then came Bob Tulius, Bob Sharp and a couple of other top local drivers.

Bob added that these guys, like him, raced every weekend while I only had been racing once a month. He told me, "You're a good steady driver and with a better car and more time on the track you'd be an asset to Group 44. I started to mention my artificial leg, but he beat me to it saying, "Yeah, so you got a wooden leg. We can build you a clutch just like Belgard did."

Boy! Was I on cloud nine. I told him I would think it over and let him know in a day or two. I had a lot of dreams of becoming a top-flight driver, winning championships and racing tracks all around the country, but then I came down to reality. This would take up most all of my time in practice, working on the car and traveling to races. There would be no time left for my six year old son who I now saw most every weekend. I divorced his mother when he was three, as she had no desire to stay at home and be a mother to my son and her daughter. The weekends with him at my parent's home was a stabilizing influence on his life, or at least I hoped it would be.

The next day I called Bob and thanked him very much for considering me for his new racing team, but I couldn't do it. I told him about my son and my parents and he understood. He also understood how much I would have liked to join Group 44. All of the Group's cars were white and when the group became successful the press dubbed them "The Great White Wave." I read much later after I had left the track that Bob and his team came in third in the Twenty Four Hours of Le Manns driving a new Jaguar. Sometimes, even forty years later I wonder if I made the right choice and wonder what it would feel like to be a retired racecar driver of national renown. However, I still have plenty of happy memories of when I was part of the racing scene.

# Chapter Twenty-Three

## Some Things That Happened on the Track

In my almost ten years of racing I never won a trophy, but did pretty good for a part time one-legged driver. Looking back, I can truly say it was the best part of my life. At least it was the most fun and all of the exercise, both working on and driving the car, kept me in good physical condition.

Here are a few things that sort of stand out in my memory of great days of racing a sports car.

I didn't have many spinouts and only one that was anywhere near spectacular. I guess that was because I had a very good feel for the "hairy edge," and always knew where the other guy was.

My worst spin out occurred as I was entering the "S" turn. I had been trying to catch and pass a Morgan for several laps and had been gaining on him. As I went over the edge of the oval and came down with a "kerplunk" at the entrance of the "S" turn I looked up for less than a second to see how far ahead of me that Morgan racecar was.

I had figured that maybe I could catch up with him as he slowed down for the hairpin turn. I would have to dive deeper into the turn than he, but my TR could do it. I only looked away for "ye ole" split second, but that was enough or perhaps I should say too much time. When my eyes returned to the track I knew I was in trouble.

I was about a foot out of my groove for the turn. My car was just past my turning point so that when I did turn, my back end came swinging around. Instead of heading on down the track I was headed for a very tall sheet metal fence that enclosed the track at this point of the road course.

It looked like that big slab of metal was falling on top of me. I made a quick turn on my steering wheel hoping I might somehow avoid smashing into or through that fence. It worked! My car, revolving like a kid's top spun toward the infield. However, it didn't get very far before it ran head on into a mound of very muddy dirt.

To say the least, there was a sudden jolt. I flung myself towards the passenger seat and held on to the grab bar. Mud went flying all over the place as the TR buried its nose in the pile of dirt. I was a little shook up, but not hurt. My seat belt had held my butt in place and my grip on that chrome handle about the glove box had worked.

I had come to rest not far from the front of the main grandstand.

I undid my seatbelt and made a one-legged jump out of the car. As I hopped to the trunk end of my car a roar went up from the crowd watching from the stands. The track announcer told me later that the audience at first thought I had lost my leg in the wreck. Sounds silly, no one had ever heard of a one-legged man driving a racecar.

There was no serious damage done to my car either. There was a lot of mud in between the grill and the radiator. I couldn't run far or fast without over heating. The mud had to come out. Ted and I tried to get the grill off, but the screws were frozen in place. I tried to find some WD-40, but no one had any.

I wished I had a fire hose. That would blast it out. I said fire hose, as I was a member of the Indian River Volunteer Fire Company. Even a garden hose would have helped. We tried throwing a few buckets of water into the grill. This helped a bit, but not enough. I took a long handled screwdriver and Ted found a slim but sturdy stick and we sat down to flick the mud out little bit by little bit. We finally go it clean enough that I could run in the final race of the day.

definitely wrong so I drove my car with its floppy clutch back to the pits.

Nobody there could help me and my mechanic Jack Belgard, had gone home for the day.

I decided that since I had driven it around the racecourse in the floppy condition, that I could drive it some forty miles home. If not maybe I could get it closer to a local tow service. (My racing budget was a very slim one.) I packed up my things and headed out of the track gate into the setting sun with my fingers crossed.

All went well until I got through Hyattsville. There, when I pushed the button I could hear the air tank hiss, but the clutch would not work. I got out and hopped around the car taking a look under the hood and saw that the vacuum part of the clutch was still working, but the swinging back and forth of the shift lever had cut through the cable that connected the clutch arm to the vacuum tank. This was the end of the ride for me.

Across the street there was a phone booth so I got out my crutches and went over to it. I first called Jack. I was lucky. He was home and answered my call. I told him what had happened and he said he would pick the car up after his dinner and let me know if he could fix it in time for tomorrow's race. I thanked him and called a cab.

I didn't make it home, but Hyattsville was only a mile or so away and was close to where my mechanic lived. The next morning Jack called me at 6:00 am. He said he was sorry, but there was no way that my TR-3 would be able to go racing. It seems that the transmission bell housing had cracked all the way around. Jack said it was not supposed to happen on the smaller sports cars like the Triumph. It seems that I had another first.

I was disappointed, but glad to hear that it was not my driving that had caused the bell housing to split. I put on my leg and went into the kitchen and cooked some bacon and eggs for breakfast. I called my Dad and told him what had happened and he lent me his Oldsmobile so I would not miss the races.

I headed out to Marlboro again this time as a spectator. I had thought of taking my camera, but was in no mood to act the photographer. Also I did not have enough film on hand. I watched the action from the pit area and spent most of my time in Dick Thompson's Corvette pits. Everyone asked me what had happened and when I told them of the split bell housing, they all said that they had never heard of such a thing in a car of my "class."

High horsepower cars like Vettes and Ferraris sometimes had this happen due to the high compression engine. I remember when Fred Windbridge had his foot injured when the clutch exploded when he was driving "The Black Beast of Foggy Bottom." This was a Lister Corvette owned by Mrs. Bowden, on of the DuPonts.

After the last race most of the drivers and car owners went into town and the Marlboro Inn for the traditional steak and French fry dinner. Dick Thompson asked me to join his table. It was quite a famous racing group including Roger Penske and Jim Hall all the way from Texas. Most every one had met me before so no introductions were necessary. I was beginning to feel like a real pro myself, but I knew my racing skill could not match any one sitting at that table.

While I was waiting for my steak, Duncan Black came over to say "Hello." At that time I did not know it but Duncan was the Black in Black & Decker tools. His grandfather had founded the company and invented the first hand held electric drill. Duncan continued by saying he was sorry to hear about my car. He added that if he had known it earlier I could have driven one of his.

Now this was a very big compliment as Mr. Black had quite a stable of expensive racecars. I thanked him but told him that I could not have driven any of them. He started to apologize, but I stopped him. I told him it was a compliment to me that he forgot that I only had one leg.

Jim Hall who had been busy demolishing his steak, they were real good T-bones, suddenly said, "Don you could have driven mine!" He meant that his Chaparral had an automatic transmission. Everyone agreed that I could drive his car as well as my Triumph with its special clutch. Actually Jim had several racecars with hydromatic transmissions in them that he was testing for General Motors.

Me, I just sat there and said something like, I guess I could.

It didn't dawn on me till later that Jim was opening a door for me and if I had said something like, "Boy I sure would like to try that", I might have been invited to go back with him to his ranch in Texas where he had his cars as well as a good sized test track of his own.

I still often wonder what it would have been like to drive one of those sleek low cars at speed. I also wondered why I did not say more as there is nothing bashful about me. However, I didn't, so it is all but a dream and a dream of yesteryears.

# Chapter Twenty-Five

## A High Class "Pit Crew"

The Washington, D.C. Region of the Sports Car Club of America usually sponsored two national meets a year at their Upper Marlboro, Maryland simulated road course. The national events attracted top drivers from all over the country and were "class" events.

This incident occurred during one of these races. It was near the end of Saturdays practice in my TR-3 that it suddenly started to misfire as I rounded "Cappy's Corner" and headed into the oval. I made it up the hump and into the oval, but there the engine stopped. I coasted around to in front of the grand stand and pulled up close to the wall and came to a halt.

I tried to restart the engine, but no luck. No matter what I tried it would not kick over. I was wondering what I was going to do as my one-man pit crew, Ted Penn, was away on an errand and would not be back for an hour or more. I started to get out of the car and hop around to the trunk for my crutches when I saw three guys

TR-3's down to a lower class where they could be in the race again. During this time formula racing had become popular. I should say with SCCA as Formula One cars and Indy cars were popular then as they are now, but were too expensive for most of us.

However, a small car called a Formula III caught my eye. It was the bottom line of the formulas, but had the thrills and great feeling of open wheel racing. They had an alcohol burning, air-cooled, one or two-cylinder motorcycle engine in the rear. When seated, ones feet went all the way out to the front of the car. On each side of the single bucket seat was a gas; I should say alcohol or fuel, tank.

It was indeed a snug fit. Sort of like wearing a car. It was fired by a motorcycle "Dirt-Track" magneto (no battery). Also the fuel pump ran off a cam on the rear axle. The fuel was pumped up to a small reserve tank just behind the driver's head so the fuel could gravity feed to the one S.V. carb and engine. This gave the car two peculiarities. One you had to push it to start it and second it did not pump fuel when the car was not moving.

The big thing that appealed to me was that there would not be any costly or complicated mechanism need for me to be able to drive it with my one good leg. The car did have a working clutch pedal on the floor in the usual location. However, since it operated a motorcycle clutch, conversion to hand use was easy. Maybe not for me, but for my mechanic an easy job. The gearbox and shift lever was on the right side of the car just above the fuel tank. A standard motorcycle clutch-operating handle was mounted on the shift lever.

This same hand squeezed lever that was on a bikes handlebar now worked the clutch on my car. The gearbox arrangement I never did like. I had always used the standard "H" pattern box with maybe reverse off to the right or left. This pattern was what they called a ratchet type with the gears all in a line.

At the bottom was reverse, then neutral, low, third and high. It worked ok for just driving, but on the track at racing speeds I was never sure what gear I was in. Of course I could tell by watching the red line on the tachometer. This was a big round dial set in the dashboard right in front of the driver. The only other "instruments" on the dash was a small red light that shined red when the oil pressure was low and a toggle switch to kill the engine.

There were two F-III owners in the D.C. Region. I had talked to Willy Gadwa about my interest. He had sold me on this little critter as a great drive! He put me in touch with Lex du Pont who was more or less the importer of this British car. He had a used Cooper Formula III available at an affordable price and soon it was mine.

Thus I became a Formula driver. It was a sensational experience. The biggest thrill I have ever had. The car held to the track like glue. That's not too good of an expression, as glue would slow down a car. However, this feeling was not evident. Going into the curves the car seemed to just flatten out.

Although the Cooper would not go as fast as my Triumph, one got the feeling of going faster. The car was small with your butt only inches from the asphalt. Also there was very little car around you. It was almost literally driving by "the seat of your pants."

The first year was great! I didn't win any races as there were more seasoned drivers (also with more money) ahead of me. I did miss the trunk that my TR had, as with the Cooper there was no place to put my crutches. They had to be left behind in my pit. This meant a lot more hopping when my car failed on the racecourse.

There is a lot more that I could write about my cars and racing experiences, but this book is supposed to be about my artificial legs and me. The open wheeled cars could not be run with the "fender types" for safety reasons. Formula III ran with its big brother, Formula Junior, a bigger, faster and more expensive vehicle.

The "Juniors" could race any distance and preferred a longer race of an hour or hour and a half. We had started running thirty-minute races that were fine for the F-III's as this car had been designed to run a short race on a small oval. The Jr's kept asking for longer races until they reached an hour to one and a half. This was the death knell for my little car. Most of the cars did not have a fuel tank large enough to go this distance. My two side tanks were ample, but the vibration of the car would shake something loose over this longer period of time no matter what one did to try and secure every little (and big) part.

Finally I looked around and discovered that I was the only alcohol burning, Formula III car still racing. There was no more F-III Class or trophy and I certainly couldn't compete with the much speedier Formula Junior cars! I too abandoned my alki burner. I sold it to a guy that turned it into some kind of dragster.

I bought an Austin Healy Sprite from a student that chickened out of driving school, but never really got to race it. SCCA came out with a mess of new rules that made my roll bar a half inch too low and they required a steel shatter shield over the clutch for all cars in spite of the power of their engines. I would also need a new high tech flameproof driver's suit, fireproof socks and a fireproof scarf over my beard.

I had been driving for ten years and was approaching fifty years of age. I did not feel that age had slowed any of my reactions, but decided that all of the new costs would be too much so I quietly retired and left sports car racing once again without a one legged driver.

ABOVE: Me in my Cooper F-III with other formula III open wheelers in the pits at Cumberland, Md., airport for the National SCCA Spring race. I'm the one in the a car and standing by my one-man pit crew Thomas Francis. BELOW: My Cooper and I at a field trial before the car got its Mobil gaspump red.

# Chapter Twenty-Seven

## Thoughts on My Artificial Legs

The basic purpose of a prosthesis, or artificial leg is to get a person walking again as close as possible in the manner he walked when he had two of his own home grown legs. The secondary purpose is for the patient to look as normal as possible. Perhaps I should say as whole as possible, but the main purpose is still to get the amputee from here to there.

The appearance is important to a certain point. Certainly no one wants to look like a cripple. In fact every one including the one who lost his leg goes a long way to avoid this word. I know I did not like to be called a cripple. However, the dictionary defines cripple as a disabled person and adds, "considered somewhat offensive term." I don't know why this should be, but it is. I don't like to be referred to as crippled even though I know that's what I am.

I am proud to be a life member of the Disabled American Veterans (DAV), but crippled American Veterans has a nasty flavor to it. I am losing the main point. Don't let any label or name affect what you do with the rest of your life, (This goes for arm amputees also), just go ahead and do the best you can, but keep on trying.

Many of the walking problems that seemed big at first soon became routine. I remember the first time I crossed a busy street in downtown Washington, D.C. When the walk signal came on, the curb on the other side of the street seemed a mile away and as high as Mount Everest. However, such street crossings soon became a routine matter.

Due to the slower gait of the artificial knee my time for crossing the street was very short. I always kept my eyes open for that guy who liked to leave like a dragster when the light turned green. For this reason I usually carried a cane when in downtown traffic. Swinging it along in front of me saved me many times from being hit by a car or run over, so to speak, by those rushing to go no where in particular on the city sidewalks.

I was lucky as for most of my one-legged life I didn't really need a cane to walk. I had a good sense of balance and tough hide covering the end of my stump. I do like canes and they tend to give me a feeling of dignity, so I often used one for just the "feel" or look of it.

I had quite a collection of them including an antique Irish blackthorn walking stick. It had belonged to my Uncle's father Mr. McCarthy who brought it with him from the old country when he immigrated to the U.S. in the early 1800's. It was a tough stick and a good defensive weapon. I always felt safe with it in my grasp no matter how dark or deserted the street that I was walking down. My infantry training and combat experience had taught me how to use such a "stick" as a weapon!

# Chapter Twenty-Eight

## Legs I Have Walked On

Most of this information has appeared in more detail in other parts of this book. I thought it might be interesting to summarize these artificial limbs as sort of a grand finale.

My first adventure at walking again was a brief one. A fellow patient at Walter Reed gave me his wooden peg leg that had been used to free his stiffened knee joint. I made a few changes in it and was having a ball walking around the ward when the head nurse intercepted me. She really dressed me down in no uncertain terms. "You will develop bad walking habits that will ruin your ability to use a proper leg when the time came!" she said.

I didn't agree with her, but she was a captain and I a private first class, so off came the peg leg and back I was on crutches. That brief period that I spent on that leg gave me a lot of confidence and I was now sure that I would do more than ok with my proper AK (above the knee) leg.

My next leg was my GI issue made for a weight-bearing stump. As mentioned before the shank part was white "plastic," and was shaped like an upside down milk bottle. The knee joint was an axle with a bit of friction applied. When I kicked my stump, so to speak, the boot part of my leg and artificial foot swung out in front of me and I stepped on it.

The "socket" where my stump went was leather that laced up the front making me take most of my body's weight on the end of my stump. I had my entire femur bone. This leg was not a thing of beauty, but it looked great to me. It also worked fine as a training leg that helped develop a new set of muscles in my thigh that grew from lifting the dead weight of my plastic lower limb.

Leg number three came about three months after my discharge from Walter Reed. It was a leg made out of willow wood custom tailored for me. I had a choice of materials for my leg, they were, wood of the willow tree that was both light and tough, aluminum, also light, in fact for my use too light. It also dented easily and was apt to make metallic noises, and plastic, this was heavier and I did not like it.

By the time I went to the Universal Artificial Limb, Company in Washington, D.C., the weight bearing type of leg had proved to be too hard on the end of the stump. My new leg had a wooden "socket" made so that I took most of my weight on the lower part of my butt and the sides of my stump. This worked a lot better. Of course it had a much bigger leather belt going around me a little below my waist to hold the leg on to me.

This belt was the most uncomfortable part of my artificial leg. It was back then and it is now. On a hot day when I was doing physical work it would get soaked with sweat and sweat soaked leather does not feel good or smell very nice either, but it worked and I learned to live and work with it.

The early foot and ankle left a lot to be desired. There was a front section for the area shaped roughly like the toes bunched together. This was joined to the back part of the wood foot with a leather hinge so the foot would bend at the "ball" of the foot when walking. The ankle was a combination of a "U" and "eye" bolt to hold the foot to the shank part of the leg and there was a solid hose like piece of rubber than ran from the foot up into the leg to give the ankle movement. There were also rubber bushings in the ankle.

All of this worked very well and gave a natural looking movement to the foot. The problem was it did not last very long particularly if one was walking around sand or dirt. I did a lot of work in and around sand both at the beach and helping my cousin build a house in the country facing on the Potomac River.

I often wore out an ankle joint over the weekend no matter how careful I tried to be. I also broke an ankle lifting weights. I don't know how much was on the bar when I made my last lift over my head. However it was enough to break the parts of my ankle so I took up other forms of exercise.

This problem was ended when the Veterans Administration Orthopedic Board asked me if I would help test a new foot. I was going to the University of Maryland at this time so I could work it into my schedule. This foot was made of sections and/or layers of tough sponge like material and smoothly attached to the ankle. There was no place for sand or grit to get in.

It was called the Sach (I'm not sure of the spelling but that's what it sounded like) foot. This was a big improvement in the artificial leg. Sand would get in my shoe, but it would only wear away my sock. That didn't bother me as I had started getting all of my socks the same color and style. I never changed the one on my artificial foot until the top pulled loose from the bottom. No one could see my bottomless sock.

The next big improvement came later and it did away with that undesirable leather belt. It was the suction socket leg. Yep! Suction held it on to your stump. There was a small lightweight emergency belt, but that was no bother at all, at least compared to the old belts.

This leg had some drawbacks, but you read about these experiences in the front part of my book.

I wore my suction socket leg as my dress leg until my arthritis moved down into my hands making it difficult and painful to pull the slip sock through the bottom hole. I had been using a peg type leg for yard work and work around the firehouse and down by my boat dock. It was easier to walk backwards without waiting for the swing of the knee joint to reach its end.

The peg leg was also a lot lighter than my plastic one. (The original willow wood had been replaced by some kind of plastic.) This was good, as old age had slowed me a bit. However, it meant back to the leather waist belt and also back to wearing stump socks.

The wearing part of the stump sock was no so bad. It made me hotter in the summertime, but it was the washing that was a pain in the . . . Well, you know where!

One disadvantage to the peg leg was that because of the lack of a knee joint, when I sat down it stuck straight out in front of me. This made sitting at the bar very difficult and in a car impossible! This problem was relieved by a separation in the leg at the end of the socket and the knee joint. The two pieces of my leg were held together by a large "plastic" screw.

This meant to sit at a bar, in a car or any tight place the leg had to be taken apart by removing the screw. The bottom of my leg, a fourteen inch pipe with a hard rubber "ball" of a foot at one end, made a good club. When sitting at a bar I put it down on the floor. Occasionally when the drinkers at the bar seemed to be getting a little rowdy my wife would reach down and grab it. Then with a couple of poundings on the bar she would say, "Let there by order!" or words to that effect. It always worked and Big Mac behind the bar put his shillelagh back in its place below the cash register and gave us both a word of thanks.

When Courtney at Universal Artificial Limb Company, first showed me this type of leg, he said that the Veterans Administration had okayed it for a couple of Viet Nam War amputees as a sports leg. It was what I had been asking about for a good many years, particularly when I was sports car racing. I wasn't racing anymore, but it would make life easier as a fireman and a member of the Coast Guard Auxiliary to say nothing about it being handy in trying to turn my backyard from a wild field of miscellaneous vegetation into some form of garden and lawn!

It seems that my peg leg, that the Veterans Administration had called a "sports leg," was now a working leg! At least that was what I used it for. I still usually wore my nicer looking suction socket leg when going out in the evenings with my wife, but that too was soon to come to an end.

One night when my wife and I were getting ready to spend an evening at my Legion Post, she said, "Honey, why don't you wear the peg leg? I bet you could dance better with it." I guess that was sort of a death knell for ye ole suction socket leg. Particularly with my arthritis making it hard and painful to get on.

The peg has been my only leg for over thirty years. It has served me well and requires a lot less maintenance. This is good for me now as my "limb man" is 150 miles away from where I live. It does not look as good as one shaped like my real leg, but I am no longer working in a "dress up" office or position.

It also seems that now in the year 2009, that people have more feeling and understanding of persons with handicaps. Little children every so often will ask me about my different kind of leg and if they are polite about it I tell how I lost it in a big war long ago. I am also careful when approaching dogs as they notice the difference right away. I move slowly and talk gently to them to let them know I am a friend.

Today's artificial limbs are high tech and seem to do wonderful things. If I were a lot younger I sure would give one a good try.

However, my "peg" still gets me from here to there with ease. I also have far less trips to the limb shop for repairs. The rubber pad on the bottom of my foot comes loose once in awhile, but a few squirts of a strong glue gets it fixed. On the new high tech legs I suspect that the computer like parts would need more maintenance, but how I don't know.

The important thing is to choose a leg that suits you. A proper fit is also necessary for good and comfortable walking.

# Many Thanks
## to

The Ladies Auxiliary and Sons of the American Legion Squadron of the Oak Orchard - Riverdale American Post 28, Millsboro, Delaware. Without their financial help and help with the typing of my manuscripts this book would not be. A special thanks to Auxiliary President Carole Baldwin, Commander Mike Cotten of the SAL Squadron, and Cindy Phillips, Auxiliary Secretary for the Auxiliary Chapter for her fine typing of my manuscript

# Other Book by Don Addor

NOVILLE Out Post of BASTONE is the story of my part in the defense of Bastogne during the Battle of the Bulge in Belgium during World War II and other battles with the 10th Armored Division, Patton's Third Army.

HALELLUJAH covers my experiences and that of my family with the miracles of our Lord. Both books are available from Trafford Publishing: 1-888-232-4444; or from the author at 503 Mulberry Street, Milton, DE 19968.